First World War
and Army of Occupation
War Diary
France, Belgium and Germany

27 DIVISION
80 Infantry Brigade
King's Royal Rifle Corps
4th Battalion
18 October 1914 - 28 October 1915

WO95/2262/1

The Naval & Military Press Ltd
www.nmarchive.com
Published in association with The National Archives

Published by

The Naval & Military Press Ltd

Unit 10 Ridgewood Industrial Park,

Uckfield, East Sussex,

TN22 5QE England

Tel: +44 (0) 1825 749494

www.naval-military-press.com

www.nmarchive.com

This diary has been reprinted in facsimile from the original. Any imperfections are inevitably reproduced and the quality may fall short of modern type and cartographic standards.

© Crown Copyright
Images reproduced by permission of The National Archives, London, England, 2015.

Contents

Document type	Place/Title	Date From	Date To
Heading	WO95/2262/1		
Heading	27th Division 80th Infy Bde 4th Bn K. R. R. C. Nov 1914-Oct 1915		
Heading	80th Infantry Brigade. 27th Division (Battn. Disembarked Havre From England 21.12.14) 4th Battn. The King's Royal Rifle Corps November & December (19.11.14 To 31.12.14) 1914		
War Diary	Mom Hill Camp Winchester	19/11/1914	19/11/1914
War Diary	Winchester	18/10/1914	20/12/1914
War Diary	Havre	21/12/1914	31/12/1914
Miscellaneous	4th Bn. King's Royal Rifle Corps.		
Miscellaneous	4th Battalion The Kings Royal Rifle Corps		
Miscellaneous	4 K. R. R. Corps Normal Roll of Officers		
Heading	80th Infantry Brigade. 27th Division. 4th Battn. The King's Royal Rifle Corps January 1915		
War Diary		01/01/1915	06/01/1915
War Diary	Elsonval	07/01/1915	07/01/1915
War Diary	St Eloi	08/01/1915	13/01/1915
War Diary	Elzonvalle	14/01/1915	17/01/1915
War Diary	Mt Kokereele	18/01/1915	28/01/1915
War Diary	St Eloi	28/01/1915	30/01/1915
War Diary	Voormezeele	31/01/1915	31/01/1915
War Diary	Dickebusch	31/01/1915	31/01/1915
Miscellaneous	Appendix A		
Operation(al) Order(s)	Operation Order No. 1 Appendix "A"	04/01/1915	04/01/1915
Operation(al) Order(s)	Operation Order No. 2 By Major B.F Widdrington Commanding 4th Bn K. R. R. C.	05/01/1915	05/01/1915
Operation(al) Order(s)	Operation Order No. 3 By Major B.F Widdrington Commanding 4th Roll The Kings Royal Rifle Corps	07/01/1915	07/01/1915
Operation(al) Order(s)	Operation Order No. 4 By Major B.F Widdrington Commanding 4th Bn. Kings Royal Rifle Corps	13/01/1915	13/01/1915
Operation(al) Order(s)	Operation Order No. 5 By Major B.F Widdrington Commanding The Kings Royal Rifle Corps	17/01/1915	17/01/1915
Operation(al) Order(s)	Operation Order No. 6 By Major B.F Widdrington Commanding 4th Bn. The Kings Royal Rifle Corps	23/01/1915	23/01/1915
Miscellaneous	Appendix B		
Miscellaneous	Casualties For The Period 7th-8th January 1915 Appendix "B"		
Miscellaneous	Casualties For The Period 28th-30th January 1915		
Miscellaneous	Appendix C		
Miscellaneous	Appendix 'C'		
Diagram etc			
Miscellaneous	Work Required		
Heading	80th Infantry Brigade. 27th Division 4th Battn. The King's Royal Rifle Corps. February 1915		
War Diary	Dickebusch	01/02/1915	02/02/1915
War Diary	Voormezeele	02/02/1915	09/02/1915
War Diary	Dickebusch	10/02/1915	10/02/1915
War Diary	Right Section 27th Div Trenches	11/02/1915	17/02/1915
War Diary	Dickebusch	18/02/1915	19/02/1915

War Diary	Elzonvalle	20/02/1915	21/02/1915
War Diary	Zevecoton	22/02/1915	27/02/1915
War Diary	Dickebusch	27/02/1915	28/02/1915
Miscellaneous	Appendix B		
Miscellaneous Heading	80th Infantry Brigade. 27th Division. 4th Battn. The King's Royal Rifle Corps March 1915		
War Diary		01/03/1915	04/03/1915
War Diary	St. Eloi	05/03/1915	05/03/1915
War Diary	Dickebusch	06/03/1915	08/03/1915
War Diary	St Eloi	09/03/1915	09/03/1915
War Diary	Dickebusch	10/03/1915	11/03/1915
War Diary	Zevecoton	12/03/1915	24/03/1915
War Diary	Near Poperinghe	25/03/1915	25/03/1915
Miscellaneous	Appendix B		
Miscellaneous			
Miscellaneous	Appendix "B"		
Miscellaneous	Appendix C		
Miscellaneous	4th Battalion The Kings Royal Rifle Corps Report Appendix "C"	03/03/1915	03/03/1915
Diagram etc	Rough Stretch To Illustrate Operations of 1st-2nd March 1914		
Diagram etc	Rough Plan of The German Trench		
Heading	80th Infantry Brigade 27th Division. 4th Battn. The King's Royal Rifle Corps. April 1915		
War Diary		04/04/1915	30/04/1915
Miscellaneous	Casualty List		
Miscellaneous Heading	80th Infantry Brigade 27th Division. 4th Battn. The King's Royal Rifle Corps May 1915		
War Diary		01/05/1915	31/05/1915
Miscellaneous	Casualty List		
Miscellaneous	Casualties 4.5.15	04/05/1915	04/05/1915
Heading	80th Infantry Brigade 27th Division 4th Battn. The King's Royal Rifle Corps June 1915		
War Diary		01/06/1915	08/06/1915
War Diary	Armentieres	08/06/1915	15/06/1915
War Diary	Near Armentieres	16/06/1915	01/07/1915
Miscellaneous	Casualty List		
Miscellaneous	12164 RFN G Wallace, Killed 2.6.1915.		
Heading	80th Infantry Brigade. 27th Division. 4th Battn. The King's Royal Rifle Corps July (1.7.15 To 1.8.15) 1915		
War Diary		01/07/1915	01/08/1915
Miscellaneous	Casualty List		
Miscellaneous	7052 RFN W Barrowcliffe Wounded 3.7.15		
Heading	80th Infantry Brigade. 27th Division. 4th Battn. The King's Royal Rifle Corps August (9.8.15 To 30.8.15) 1915		
War Diary	Near Armentieres	09/08/1915	30/08/1915
Miscellaneous	Casualty List		
Miscellaneous	Casualties For Period 1st To 31st August 1915		
Heading	80th Infantry Brigade. 27th Division. 4th Battn. The King's Royal Rifle Corps. September (31.8.15 To 30.9.15) 1915		
War Diary		31/08/1915	14/09/1915
War Diary	Strazeele	18/09/1915	30/09/1915

Miscellaneous	Casualty List		
Miscellaneous	Casualties For Period 1st To 30th September 1915		
Heading	80th Infantry Brigade. 27th Division. 4th Battn. The King's Royal Rifle Corps. October 1915		
War Diary	Frise	01/10/1915	01/10/1915
War Diary	Froissy	02/10/1915	09/10/1915
War Diary	Frise	09/10/1915	09/10/1915
War Diary	Cappy	11/10/1915	11/10/1915
War Diary	Morcourt	13/10/1915	20/10/1915
War Diary	Trenches	21/10/1915	21/10/1915
War Diary	Froissy	22/10/1915	25/10/1915
War Diary	Warfusee-Abancourt	26/10/1915	26/10/1915
War Diary	Boves	27/10/1915	27/10/1915
War Diary	Revelles	28/10/1915	28/10/1915
Miscellaneous	Appendix B		
Miscellaneous	Appendix B Casualties Up To 30/11/1915	30/11/1915	30/11/1915

No 95/2262/1

27TH DIVISION
80TH INFY BDE

4TH BN K. R. R. C.
~~DEC~~ 1914-OCT 1915
NOV

80th Infantry Brigade.

27th Division.

(Battn. disembarked Havre from England 21.12.14)

WAR DIARY

4th BATTN. THE KING'S ROYAL RIFLE CORPS.

NOVEMBER & DECEMBER

(19.11.14 to 31.12.14)

1 9 1 4

Army Form C. 2118.

WAR DIARY
or
INTELLIGENCE SUMMARY

(Erase heading not required.)

Hour, Date, Place	Summary of Events and Information	Remarks and references to Appendices
Morn Hill Camp Winchester. 19-11-14	The Battalion arrived from PLYMOUTH port of disembarkation, in two trains at 8.30 a.m. After Breakfasts at the Rifle Depot proceeded to camp. The Battalion was taken on the Strength of the 80th Infantry Brigade. Commander - Brigadier General The Hon C. G. FORTESCUE CB, CMG, DSO. Brigade Major - Major R A K STEWART; K.O.S.B.	

1247 W 3299 200,000 (E) 8/14 J.B.C. & A. Forms/C.2118/11.

WAR DIARY
or
INTELLIGENCE SUMMARY
(Erase heading not required.)

Hour, Date, Place	Summary of Events and Information	Remarks and references to Appendices
WINCHESTER 18th Oct 1914	On the night of 18th/19th the issue of clothing & new Rifles was commenced. This was completed so far as Rifles & serge clothing was concerned on 19th. From this date onwards the work of placing the Battalion on a war footing both in Personnel & material was gradually proceeded with.	

WAR DIARY
or
INTELLIGENCE SUMMARY

(Erase heading not required.)

Instructions regarding War Diaries and Intelligence Summaries are contained in F.S. Regs., Part II. and the Staff Manual respectively. Title pages will be prepared in manuscript.

Hour, Date, Place	Summary of Events and Information	Remarks and references to Appendices
	Carried on –	
	The men were allowed on furlough at the rate of 20% at a time up to	
WINCHESTER Tuesday 15th Dec 1914		
16th December 1914.	The 27th Div was inspected by H.M. The King on FAWLEY DOWN.	Whvouly

WAR DIARY
or
INTELLIGENCE SUMMARY

(Erase heading not required.)

Hour, Date, Place	Summary of Events and Information	Remarks and references to Appendices
Winchester 20-12-1914. 9 a.m.	The battalion paraded and marched to SOUTHAMPTON and there entrained. The entrainment being complete except for one G.S. wagon & pair of blankets and two pairs of horses which broke down and failed to arrive in time.	
7 p.m.	Sailed in S.S. HUANCHACO together with 364th Battery R.F.A.	
HAVRE. 21-12-1914 1 p.m.	Arrives alongside quay at HAVRE and started disembarking at once. Were found the deficiency of wagon blankets and horses.	

WAR DIARY
or
INTELLIGENCE SUMMARY

(Erase heading not required.)

Instructions regarding War Diaries and Intelligence Summaries are contained in F. S. Regs., Part II. and the Staff Manual respectively. Title pages will be prepared in manuscript.

Hour, Date, Place	Summary of Events and Information	Remarks and references to Appendices
HAVRE. 22-12-14	Marched at 3-30 p.m. to the GARE DES MARCHANDISES and there entrained.	
8.15 a.m.	Routes for detraining + places of concentration not yet known.	
23-12-1914. 6 a.m.	Arrived at AIRE and proceeded to billets near BLARINGHEM.	[signature]
24-12-1914. 10-30 a.m.	Moved to BLARINGHEM into fresh billets.	
25.12.1914.	Xmas Day — remaining in billets no work being done.	[signature]

Army Form C. 2118.

(6)

WAR DIARY
or
INTELLIGENCE SUMMARY

(Erase heading not required.)

Instructions regarding War Diaries and Intelligence Summaries are contained in F. S. Regs., Part II. and the Staff Manual respectively. Title pages will be prepared in manuscript.

Hour, Date, Place	Summary of Events and Information	Remarks and references to Appendices
28th Oct e. – 31st Oct e. 1914.	The Battalion were employed during this period in digging a line of trenches in the neighbourhood of BLARINGHEM, under the direction of the G.O.C. 27th Division.	Arthur Capstaff

4th. Bn. KING'S ROYAL RIFLE CORPS.

Strength.   32 Officers.   682 Other Ranks.
Ration Strength.   21 Officers   630 O.R.

History.

The men are drawn from the MANCHESTER and BIRMINGHAM Districts.

The Battalion was in FRANCE from November 1914 to November 1915 and took part in various engagements, including the Second Battle of YPRES.   SALONICA November 1915 to June 1918, mostly on the STRUMA Front.

The system of defence on this front was chiefly a series of Redoubts and Battalion and Company raids over a distance of some miles were made from the cover of these redoubts.   Battle Casualties were very few.

(a). Health.   At present 30 - 40 cases of sickness per day, chiefly recurrent Malaria.

Transport.

Horses, Riding.	2.
" Heavy Draught.	9.
Mules, Draught.	28.
" Pack.	7.
Limbers G.S.	10.
Field Kitchens.	4.
Water Carts.	2.
Officers Mess Carts.	1.
Maltese Carts.	1.
Bicycles.	5.

Leave.   Leave Return of Other Ranks of Battalion and Nominal Roll of Officers with record of services attached.

4th Battalion The Kings Royal Rifle Corps

Numbers of N.C.O.'s who have had no leave for 3 months & upwards

Month	No. of Months	No. of O.R.
June 1917	13 x	469
May 1917	14	463
April	15	440
March	16	438
February	17	434
January	18 x	426
December 1916	19	355
November	20	355
October	21	348
September	22	326
August	23	281
July	24 x	249
June	25	225
May	26	225
April	27	225
March	28	225
February	29	225
January	30	225
December 1915	31	219
November	32	219
October	33	205
September	34	195
August	35	174
July	36 x	150
June	37	102
May	38	40

4 K.R.R. Corps.

Nominal Roll of Officers.

Name	Date of last leaving England	Substantive Rank	Date 1st Commn	Remarks
Lt. Col. M. L. S. Clements	30.1.16	Major 4.5.16	4.5.01 Reg.	At present in hospital.
Major G. A. Tryon M.C.	12.6.17	Captain 28.9.14	28.9.14 S.R.	2nd in Command
Capt. M. R. Buller	19.4.17	Captain 25.8.16	23.1.14 Reg.	
Capt. G. F. Hayhurst France M.C.	8.5.18	Captain 1.1.17	1.10.14 Reg.	
Capt. M. E. Antrobus	22.7.17	Captain 1.1.17	15.8.14 Reg.	In hospital
Capt. C. Smith	22.7.17	Captain 11.10.17	15.12.14 Reg.	
Capt. R. J. Truter M.C.	On leave in U.K.	Captain 24.2.18	28.12.14 Temp.	
Lieut. A. K. H. Wyndham	On leave in U.K.	Lieut. 14.12.15	14.8.14 S.R.	
Lieut. W. J. C. Macaulay	3.12.17	Lieut. 22.6.16	26.1.15 S.R.	
Capt. E. A. B. Miller	On leave in U.K.	Lieut. 23.10.16	17.4.15 Reg.	Adjutant
Lieut. E. C. H. Hardy	On leave in U.K.	Lieut. 10.4.17	29.10.15 Temp.	
Lieut. L. S. Burgoyne	On leave in U.K.	Lieut. 1.7.17	3.3.15 S.R.	
Lieut. O. P. Walker	22.7.17	Lieut. 1.7.17	16.3.15 S.R.	
Lieut. A. d'Argenton	On leave U.K.	Lieut. 1.7.17	16.5.15 S.R.	
Lieut. A. R. Preece	22.7.17	Lieut. 1.7.17	21.9.15 S.R.	
Lieut. M. F. Holgate	6.7.16	Lieut. 1.7.17	29.5.15 S.R.	4 E. Surreys. In hospital.
Lieut. G. K. Wells M.C.	12.2.17	Lieut. 23.9.17	23.3.16 Reg.	
Lieut. P. G. C. Debnam	12.3.17	Lieut. 22.10.17	22.4.16 Temp.	

Name	Date of last leaving England	Substantive Rank	Date of 1st Commn.	Remarks
Lieut. A.J.A Kerr	26.10.16	Lieut 7.1.18	7.7.16 S.R.	3rd Dorsets
Lieut. W.W. Wees Collins	26.10.16	Lieut 19.1.18	19.7.16 Reg.	Dorset Rgt
2 Lt. E.C.F. Munnions	26.2.17		19.12.16 Temp.	In hospital
2 Lt. H.N. Davies	22.7.17		27.3.17 Temp.	
2 Lt. H.P.L. Jollys	22.7.17		28.3.17 Temp.	
2 Lt. J. Barton	22.7.17		28.3.17 Temp.	
2 Lt. H.S. Bennett	22.7.17		28.3.17 Temp.	
2 Lt. R.E. Crosby	22.7.17		28.3.17 Temp.	
2 Lt. W.A. Fryer	22.7.17		28.3.17 Temp.	
2 Lt. J.F. Mackay	20.11.17		29.8.17 Temp.	
2 Lt. G.S. Honeycombe	31.12.17		29.8.17 Temp.	
2 Lt. W. Methven	28.12.17		28.8.17 Temp.	
Capt. Q.M. T. Jones	On leave U.K.	Hon. Capt. 1.7.7	4.1.11 Reg.	
Capt. G.J.B. Edmonds	—	Medical Officer		

Total Present	On leave	In Hospital	Total
21	7	3	32
1 (attd R.A.M.C.)			

80th Infantry Brigade.
27th Division.

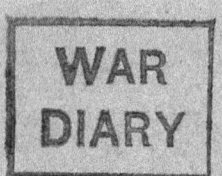

4th BATTN. THE KING'S ROYAL RIFLE CORPS.

J A N U A R Y

1 9 1 5

Attached:

Appendices
A, B and C.

4th Battalion The King's Royal Rifle Corps.

January 1915

1st Jan. 1915.

Major Widdrington (C.O.) & Major Bircham with two N.C.O's returned from the trenches where they had paid a visit of 24 hours to gain experience. In the morning the Battalion was employed in digging trenches. In the afternoon Field Marshal Sir J. D. P. French, G.C.B. Commanding in Chief

Army Form C. 2118.

(7)

WAR DIARY
or
INTELLIGENCE SUMMARY
(Erase heading not required.)

Instructions regarding War Diaries and Intelligence Summaries are contained in F. S. Regs., Part II. and the Staff Manual respectively. Title pages will be prepared in manuscript.

Hour, Date, Place	Summary of Events and Information	Remarks and references to Appendices
	inspected 70-80 th Infantry Bde.	Helmony Cappelage
2-1-15.	Battalion employed on Trench digging. Captains C. V. L. Poë & G. Wynne Finch with two N.C.O's proceeded to the Front to visit the Trenches.	
3-1-15	Again employed digging Trenches	
4-1-15.	The Battalion marched out of Billets as if moving to a new place, distance about 10 miles.	Helmony Cappelage
5-1-15	marched to CAESTRE distance about 10 miles — a considerable number of men unable to march owing to	

WAR DIARY or INTELLIGENCE SUMMARY

Army Form C. 2118.

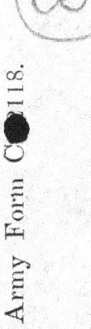

Hour, Date, Place	Summary of Events and Information	Remarks and references to Appendices
	The very bad state of the boots — On the night of 5-1-15 Brigade H.Q. were at METEREN	See Operation Order No 1 of 4.1.15 - Appendix "A" Schmauf Lyppens
6th Jan 1915	Marched from CAESTRE starting at 9.15 a.m. to a position at ELSONVAL about 1½ miles in rear of the French held by the French 32nd Division and there went into billets in the ruined houses. There was a good deal of trouble on the road owing to both troops and transport clashing with (British + French troops taking part in their relief) The Battalion went into Billets for the remainder of the	

WAR DIARY or INTELLIGENCE SUMMARY

Army Form C. 2118.

(9)

(Erase heading not required.)

Hour, Date, Place	Summary of Events and Information	Remarks and references to Appendices
7-1-15. ELSONVAL	night - and the following day. During the day there was promiscuous shell fire chiefly directed at a French battery which the Germans knew to be located somewhere in rear of ELSONVAL. Their guns frequently searched the wood about 300 yds behind ELSONVAL but failed to locate the battery.	Lieut Montfort Capt Colyt
5.0. P.M.	The Battalion started to ST ELOI a distance of about 1½ miles to take over a section of trenches held by the French. The Battalion actually took over the ST ELOI section held by the 2nd Battalion 143rd Regiment. The relief was carried out + completed by 10.30. p.m. There were there slight casualties (right half of 7-8th) Sniping continued throughout the night owing to this being the first night that the British had taken over.	See Appendix "B"

Army Form C. 2118.

WAR DIARY
or
INTELLIGENCE SUMMARY

(Erase heading not required.)

Hour, Date, Place	Summary of Events and Information	Remarks and references to Appendices
8-1-15 ST ELOI	The Frenchmen had a very difficult time carrying up enormous stores of ammunition, brassine, entrenching tools etc. A large amount of these were lost in the mud and never recovered. The position of the left company "C" was not very satisfactorily settled owing to there being a gap between their left platoon where captain McClements was situated & the remainder of the Company. Touch was correctly gained on its left with the French 142nd Regt. Promiscuous shell fire was carried on during the morning. At about 11.20 a.m. the village was bombarded fairly heavily for about twenty minutes. One horrible high explosive shell dropped just outside the cellar in which battalion headquarters were situated & partially & blowing in a built up window commend the C.O's bright in the rock. Another unfortunately found one	Vide Report on the St E401 Section of Trenches Appendix "C"

Army Form C. 2118.

WAR DIARY
or
INTELLIGENCE SUMMARY

(Erase heading not required.)

Instructions regarding War Diaries and Intelligence
Summaries are contained in F. S. Regs., Part II.
and the Staff Manual respectively. Title pages
will be prepared in manuscript.

Hour, Date, Place	Summary of Events and Information	Remarks and references to Appendices
9-1-15 ST ELOI	of the dug outs occupied by D Coy in support + killed six N.C.O's + Riflemen. Casualties for the period 7th – 8th. 9 killed + 8 wounded	
	Telephonic communication has been extremely difficult both to the Trenches + to Bde Headquarters – The wire was insufficiently insulated, surroundings wet and it rather was frequently broken by shell fire. From 1.50 P.M. to 2-25 P.M. the vicinity was bombarded by the howitzer + also by field guns with shrapnel. At 2.p.m communication was broken with Bde head Quarters and before 15 end of the bombardment all communication was cut off. By 8.p.m. all communication was restored except to "C"Coy	Appendix "B" ?
5. 20. P.M. –	Five Officers of the Cameron Highlanders arrived to be shown round the Trenches, which they were to take over on the following day —	

Army Form C.2118.

WAR DIARY
or
INTELLIGENCE SUMMARY

(Erase heading not required.)

Hour, Date, Place	Summary of Events and Information	Remarks and references to Appendices
10-1-15.	Throughout the day aeroplanes were very active. Casualties 1 killed, 7 wounded. Bombardment commenced at 9.0 a.m with the usual Howitzer which got the range of the Artillery observation post and rendered it almost untenable. Bombardment continued in-termittently until 4.0 p.m. making the position quite uncomfortable. At 6.0 p.m The Cameron Highlanders first company started the relief which was completed shortly before midnight. The Battalion moved by companies to DICKEBUSH into billets. Brig Headquarters, the last to leave arriving about 2.30 a.m 11.1.15. Three days on and in the trenches was much too long a period the result being that the battalion had almost 400 men rendered non effective by reason of frostbite, swollen feet etc. — Casualties 4 killed 6 wounded.	See Appendix B

Army Form C. 2118.

WAR DIARY
or
INTELLIGENCE SUMMARY
(Erase heading not required.)

Hour, Date, Place	Summary of Events and Information	Remarks and references to Appendices
11-1-15.	Remained in billets at DICKEBUSCH until 6.15 p.m. being in support. At the above hour being relieved by the Leinster Regiment 1st Battalion marched to billets about 1½ miles west of WESTOUTRE arriving about 11 p.m. About 150 men were admitted to hospital owing to the state of their feet this day and a further twelve wagon loads were brought to the new billets unable to march.	
12-1-15.	Remained in billets in Mt KOKEREELE - The result of the three days in the trenches is that the battalion is reduced in fighting strength to 500 of all ranks. In addition to the two officers wounded the preceding ones admitted to hospital - Capt. G. Wynne Finch -	

Army Form C. 2118.

(19)

WAR DIARY
or
INTELLIGENCE SUMMARY
(Erase heading not required.)

Instructions regarding War Diaries and Intelligence Summaries are contained in F. S. Regs., Part II. and the Staff Manual respectively. Title pages will be prepared in manuscript.

Hour, Date, Place	Summary of Events and Information	Remarks and references to Appendices
13th Jan 1915	Capt. M.L.S. Clements — Lt. S.H. Ferrand — Lt. C.S. Price — Davies — 2Lt. G.B. Eden. The Brigade marched to DICKEBUSCHE its battalion finding the Advanced Guard and moving on that night to ELZONVALLE and there taking over from the Argyll & Sutherland Highlanders & coming under the orders of the 82nd Brigade. The place had been much tidied up since we took it over from the French.	
14th Jan 1915 ELZONVALLE	During the day the battalion remained in support. The Batteries behind us were much shelled by shrapnel T howitzer but the buildings of ELZONVALLE were left alone.	

WAR DIARY or INTELLIGENCE SUMMARY

Army Form C. 2118.

(20)

Hour, Date, Place	Summary of Events and Information	Remarks and references to Appendices
15-1-15.	Rations having arrived by 6.15 p.m. the Battalion started to relieve the Leinster Regt in the ST ELOI Trenches. The relief was not finished until after midnight. Casualties —. Headquarters of battalion had during the night been established in VERMEZEELE near the dressing station. On this night the Battalion were relieved by the P.P.C.L.I. An enterprise had been planned against a German Sap jointly with the above regiment but owing to a slight misunderstanding it was not carried out, the C.O.s deciding that unless everything was absolutely correct a night operation had better not be attempted. The Battalion then fell back into support at ELZENVALLE. The relief being completed soon after midnight.	

Army Form C. 2118.

(21)

WAR DIARY
or
INTELLIGENCE SUMMARY

(Erase heading not required.)

Instructions regarding War Diaries and Intelligence Summaries are contained in F. S. Regs., Part II. and the Staff Manual respectively. Title pages will be prepared in manuscript.

Hour, Date, Place	Summary of Events and Information	Remarks and references to Appendices
16th Jan 1915	Remained in support at ELZONYALLE.	 Holman Capt & Adjt
17th Jan 1915	" " " " until Relieved at about 8 p.m by the 2nd Leinster Regt. Battalion marched undefended to Mt KOKERELLE arriving about 12.20 a.m. 18-1-15.	
18th Jan/15. Mt KOKERELLE	Remained in reserve & sent the Battalion by detachments to Mt Rouge, BOESCHEPPE to get a wash and a change of shirt & socks.	
18th to 23rd Jan.	Rest'd in BOESCHEPPE. Route marched on 20th & 22nd to keep the men fit. Numbers continue to be admitted to hospital	

Army Form C. 2118.

WAR DIARY
or
INTELLIGENCE SUMMARY

(Erase heading not required.)

Instructions regarding War Diaries and Intelligence Summaries are contained in F. S. Regs., Part II. and the Staff Manual respectively. Title pages will be prepared in manuscript.

(22)

Hour, Date, Place	Summary of Events and Information	Remarks and references to Appendices
	with bad feet & diarrhoea.	
23-1-16 - 3.20 P.M.	Started in march for DICKEBUSCH receiving orders at the last moment to go on to the Chateau near KRUISSTRAATHOEK to remain in support for the night.	
	A number of men about 65 who were marching in rear of the Battalion were stopped by the G.O.C. Division in WESTOUTRE & ordered to go back to the composite battalion in BOESCHEPPE. Spent the night in improving dug outs etc in the grounds of the Chateau	
24-1-16.	Moved at daylight to DICKEBUSCH & remained in Bivouac there during the day, going to ELZONVALLE at night.	
25-1-16 } 26-1-16 }	Remained in support of the Irish Brigade (22nd) at ELZONVALLE until dawn on 27th. There being some kind of an idea that perhaps ST. ELOI was going to be attacked.	

Army Form C. 2118.

(23)

WAR DIARY
or
INTELLIGENCE SUMMARY
(Erase heading not required.)

Instructions regarding War Diaries and Intelligence Summaries are contained in F. S. Regs., Part II. and the Staff Manual respectively. Title pages will be prepared in manuscript.

Hour, Date, Place	Summary of Events and Information	Remarks and references to Appendices
27 – 1 – 15	During the nights the battalion found fatigue parties carrying material into the trenches & other parties digging a second line of trenches in rear of YPRES. BEYOND VOORMEZEELE. At daybreak (about 6.30.a.m.) the battalion moved into DICKE-BUSCH and went into billets. Before dark C & D Coys under Captain Poë were sent to BELLEGOED CHATEAU to remain in close support until daybreak 28th.	
28 – 1 – 15	Captain Poë's detachment returned at daybreak. The battalion rested in DICKEBUSCH until evening when it proceeded to ST ELOI and took over the trenches of the Royal Irish Regt. A Coy were unfortunately badly led by a guide of	

Army Form C. 2118.

(24)

WAR DIARY
or
INTELLIGENCE SUMMARY
(Erase heading not required.)

Hour, Date, Place	Summary of Events and Information	Remarks and references to Appendices
ST ELOI 28-1-15.	71st Regiment. The moon was very bright & the guide lead them right out across the open. Fire was suddenly opened on them and they suffered twelve casualties instantly. Captain Wingfield the company commander was slightly wounded and, finding an old French near by, he ordered the remainder of the company to roll into this & decided to wait until daylight to complete the relief. This was completed about dawn without further enuf. Casualties - Company - Casualties 6 killed - 1 officer & 10 wounded	Appendix B
29-1-15	The morning passed without event. About 1.0 P.M to 2.P.M the enemy bombarded the section of French	

WAR DIARY or **INTELLIGENCE SUMMARY**

Army Form C. 2118.

(25)

Hour, Date, Place	Summary of Events and Information	Remarks and references to Appendices
ST. ELOI 30-1-14	Trenches adjoining on left with high explosive shell. They succeeded in blowing in some 30-40 yds of the French & causing about 20 casualties, fires the French to evacuate this part of the line. At dusk the French immediately reoccupied this part & started to put it into a state of defence. Towards midnight heavy firing (gun & rifle) was heard in the TROIS ROIS section but it died down in about a quarter of an hour. 2/Lt L.H.S.? A Kemp was very slightly wounded in the forearm during the night in the Trench. Casualties. 4 killed - 1 officer & 3 wounded. This day passed without much incident, there being a few casualties in the Trenches during the small hours of the	Appendix B.

WAR DIARY or INTELLIGENCE SUMMARY

Army Form C. 2118.

Hour, Date, Place	Summary of Events and Information	Remarks and references to Appendices
VOORMEZEELE 31-1-15	Morning. After dark. the Battalion was relieved by the P.P.C.L.I. in the trenches + retired to VOORMEZEELE so as to remain in close support. A + B Coys under Major Birchcliffe remained until 6.30. a.m. 31-1-15 digging in the CRIMEAN TRENCH to the West of ST ELOI and the new redoubt to the rear. Casualties - 2 Killed + 7 wounded. A draft of 78 MCOs + RPs was brought by Lt H.O.Curtis. The Battalion Remained in Support until evening when it was relieved by the 4th B. Rif. Bde. The village was capably shelled during the day most of the shots going over.	Nil Capnract[?] See Appendix "B".

Army Form C. 2118.

(27)

WAR DIARY
or
INTELLIGENCE SUMMARY

(Erase heading not required.)

Instructions regarding War Diaries and Intelligence Summaries are contained in F. S. Regs., Part II. and the Staff Manual respectively. Title pages will be prepared in manuscript.

Hour, Date, Place	Summary of Events and Information	Remarks and references to Appendices
31-1-15. DICKEBUSCH	After dusk the Battalion moved back to DICKE-BUSCH & went into billets	

A P P E N D I X   A.

Appendix 'A'

1.

Operation Order No 31
by
Major. B. F. Widdrington - Commanding 4ᵗʰ K.R.R.C.
4ᵗʰ Jan - 1915.

Ref HAZEBROUCK MAP 1/100000.

—

1. The Battalion will march in Brigade tomorrow to CAESTRE, about 10 miles. where it will billet.

Route - SERCUS — HAZEBROUCK — LE BREARD — CAESTRE.

Head of the main body will pass the starting point, D Coy's headquarters, at 9.15 A.M.

Order of march. D, A, B, C, MG sections, First line transport, Second Line Transport less supply wagons. The supply wagons will after refilling follow the column under the orders of the Bde Supply Officer.

Blanket Wagon of Right half Battⁿ will be at the Church at 8.0 A.M. and after loading by a Coy will be conducted to B Coy's loading point by a N.C.O of B. Coy.

Blanket Wagon of Left half Battⁿ will be at the road Junction immediately E. of Bⁿ Headquarters at 8.0.a.m.

Officers valises to HQʳˢ at 8.30 A.M.

Headquarter blankets will be loaded by 7.30 a.m. being divided equally between the two wagons.
All men who in the opinion of the O.C Coys are unfit to march with the Battalion owing to bad boots etc will form up in rear of the M.G. Scots under an officer to be detailed by the O.C "C" Coy.
"C" Coy will be prepared to act as Rear Guard to the Brigade if required.

        H Ponsonby Captain
    The Kings Royal Rifle Corps
      Adjutant 4th Battalion

Issued to Orderly Sergts.
at 7.50 p.m.

4

Operation Order. No 2
by.
Major. B. F Widdrington – Commanding 4"Th" K.R.R.C.
5th Jan 1915.

Ref. HAZEBROUCK MAP 1/100000.

1. The Battalion will march tomorrow to DICKE-BUSCH about 14 miles.

Order of march — A, B, C, D – M G Scots First line Tpt (less 1 Limbered wagon) 2nd Line Tpt (less Supply wagons)

Head of the main body to pass the starting point (CAESTRE CHURCH) at 9.15. a.m.

Blanket wagon of Right half batt'ns will be at the FACTORY (B Coy's billet) at 8.0 a.m.

Blanket wagon of left half batt'ns will be at the CHATEAU (D Coy's billets) at 7.45 a.m and must be loaded in time to return to "C" Coy's billets at 8.30. a.m.

Headquarters will load their blankets on these two Wagons by 7.15 a.m.

Supply wagons will leave Headquarters at 7.0 a.m. and proceed under the orders of the Quartermaster to METEREN.

Baggage + supply wagons will be handed over

5

to O.C. 96 Coy A.S.C. at the Junction of the BORRE — BAILLEUL and METEREN — BAILLEUL Road. ½ mile west of BAILLEUL Officers ralines to the transport wagons near the church, CAESTRE, at 8.30 a.m.

Men unfit to march owing to faulty boots will parade at the church, CAESTRE, at 8.0 a.m. under 2Lt C. SMITH and proceed direct to METEREN where boots will be issued to them by the Quartermaster.

After issue they will rejoin their companies etc, as the battalion marches through MET-EREN.

C.Q.M. Sgts will accompany this party with rolls of men requiring boots.

McPherson Capt.
The Kings Royal Rifle Corps.
Adjutant 1st Batt.

Issued to Orderly Sergts
at 11.0 P.M.

6

Operation Order N° 3
by
Major B F Widdrington Commanding
4th Battⁿ The King's Royal Rifle Corps
7 - 1 - 15.

1. Intention — The battalion will carry out the relief of certain trenches occupied by a part of the 32nd French Division.

2. Relief — The relief will take place as under
Front Line :- A, B & C Coys.
Support   D Coy.
All companies will march via the X roads at KRUISSTRAATHOEK passing that point at :-   A Coy 5.30 P.M
        D Coy 5.45 " "
        B Coy 6.0 " "
        C Coy 6.30 " "
M.G. 1 Section with B Coy
   1 " " D Coy
Each man will carry 250 rounds of ammunition.
O.Cs B & D Coys will arrange to help the M.G. Sections to take up their ammunition.

7

Each company will take up a proportion of the battalion tools.

O.C. Coys will arrange to take what braziers, sacks, fuel, fascines or other useful material that they can manage to carry up.

Coats will be worn & the waterproof sheet & fur waist coat will be carried in the pack.

Scouts will be distributed as under.
Two per company & Sgt Newham to go first to their trenches to learn their position & then to report to headquarters. They will sleep by day with D. Coy.

L/C Stevenson + 4 Rfm with A. Coy to keep up communication with the regiment on the right.

Cpl Hackney + 4 Rfm with C Coy to lie in the ⅔ French trench on the left of our line.

3 Reports — Reports to headquarters at the X roads ST ELOI.

Verbally to officers at 10. P.M.

H. Ponsonby Capt.
The Kings Royal Rifle Corps
Adjutant 4th Batt

Operation Order No. 4.
by.
Major B. F. Widdrington Commanding,
4th. Bn: King's Royal Rifle Corps.
13th January 1915.

Reference map 28 $\frac{1}{40000}$.

1. The Brigade has been ordered to march to DICKEBUSCH. The battalion has been detailed as advance guard and will continue its march direct to PLAS-ELZONVALLE and come under the orders of the G.O.C., 82nd Infantry Brigade

2. Order of march of Brigade
Advanced Guard Commander:—
Major B. F. Widdrington
4th. Bn. K.R.R.Corps.

3. Main Body.
2nd K.S.L.I.
4th. R.B
3rd. K.R.R.C.
P.P.C.L.I.

4. Starting point for battalion
The road junction leading down to "A" Coy's billets at 2 p.m., at which hour the head of the main body

of the battalion will pass.

Order of march of battalion
"C" Van guard.
"D" ⎫
"A" ⎬ Main body.
"B" ⎭

Route.   WESTOUTRE — X Roads M 17 —
LA CLYTTE — DICKEBUSCH — ELZONVALLE

H. C. Powson, Captain,
The King's Royal Rifle Corps.
Adjutant, 4th Battalion.

Issued to Orderly Sergts.
at 11.10 am.

Operation Order No. 5.
by
Major B. F. Widdrington,
The King's Royal Rifle Corps,
Commanding 4th Battalion.

19th January 1915.

Reference Sheet 28 $\frac{1}{40000}$.

1. The Brigade on relief this evening will march to WESTOUTRE and remain in reserve. Battalions will march independently when relieved.

Route :- DICHEBUSCH - X Roads S.E. of H32 - OUDERDOM to billets.

Order of march :- D. A. B. C.

As soon as the relieving battalions arrives, Companies will fall in and report when they are ready to march.

'A' Coy. will join the column at the cross roads immediately N.W. of their billets.

All Coys. will send guides to meet the incoming battalion at the above X roads.

H. Howson, Captain
The King's Royal Rifle Corps,
Adjutant, 4th Battalion.

Issued to Ord. Sgts.
at 1 p.m.

Operation Order No. 6.

by.

Major B. F. Widdrington, Commanding

4th Bn. The King's Royal Rifle Corps.

23rd January 1915.

Reference map 28 1/40000.

1. The Brigade will march today to DICKEBUSCH
Order of march.

(a) Advance guard Commander

Col. Bridgford 2nd K.S.L.I.

2nd. K.S.L.I.

(b).

Main body in order of march.

4th. R.B.
P.P.C.L.I.
4th. K.R.R.C.
3rd. K.R.R.C.

Route:— WESTOUTRE — CROSS ROADS Sq. M.
17 — LA CLYTTE.

2. The battalion will march as under.
The head of the battalion passing the starting
point at 3-20 p.m.

Order of march:— C.D.A.B.

Starting point the road junction

immediately EAST of "A" Company's billet
2nd Line Transport has marched under
special instructions.

H.W. Parsons, Captain,
The King's Royal Rifle Corps,
Adjutant, 4th Battalion.

Dictated to Orderly Sergeants at 10 a.m.

APPENDIX B.

APPENDIX "B".

Casualties for the period 7th -8th January 1015.

No.	Rank.	Name	Nature of Casualty.	Remarks.
8481	L/c	Langabeer J	Killed	
8945	"	Harding F	"	
7117	Rfn.	Allen G	"	
7704	"	Elsdon F	"	
7141	Bugr	White H	"	
9163	Rfn	Wood J	"	
1884	"	Speed J	"	
10081	"	White A	"	
10238	"	Counter H	"	
9877	L/c	Brown H	Wounded	
10417	"	Nelson R	"	
7954	Rfn	Shepherd A	"	
9204	"	Conway W	"	
Y564	"	Wood A	"	
6970	Sgt	Williams A	"	
9302	Rfn	Thompson R	"	
Y927	"	Tansley J	"	
3448	Bugr	Dickinson A	"	

Casualties 9th January 1915.

No.	Rank.	Name	Nature of Casualty.	Remarks.
10178	L/c	Jeynes F	Killed.	
	2nd Lieutenant	Morgan H.W.	Wounded	
10098	L/c	Boxall A	"	
8799	"	Clayton E	"	
9157	Rfn	Childs G	"	
8850	"	Oxley B	"	
	2nd Lieutenant	Madeley	"	
8531	Cpl	Donnelly A	"	

Casualties 10th January 1915.

No.	Rank.	Name	Nature of Casualty.	Remarks.
8543	Cpl	Burton F	Killed.	
9862	"	Harrow J	"	
9921	Rfn	Brennan F	"	
8728	"	Sutton H	"	
7591	"	Smith F	Wounded.	
8466	L/c	Fletcher E	"	
6871	Rfn	Hooton T	"	
8505	"	Leach E	"	
8120	"	Nield H	"	
8745	"	Penkethman J	"	

Casualties 15th January 1915.

No.	Rank.	Name	Nature of Casualty.	Remarks.
7699	Rfn	Kingston F	Killed	
7166	"	Rowe J	Wounded	
7821	"	Evans J	"	
9344	L/c	Dobson R	"	
6903	Rfn	Spears G	"	
7939	"	Crittenden W	"	
7884	"	Rumbles A	"	
7052	"	Barrowcliffe W	"	
9255	"	Addison A	"	
7796	"	Richardson A	"	
10090	C			

Casualties 16th January 1915.

No.	Rank.	Name	Nature of Casualty.	Remarks.
10090	Rfn	Collins W	Wounded.	
	Lieutenant	Curtis H.O.	"	

To date:- Killed 15. Wounded, officers 3, Others 30.

Casualties for the period 28th - 30th January 1915.

No.	Rank	Name	Nature of Casualty	Remarks
9351	L/c	Walton C	Killed.	28/1/1915.
9892	Rfn	Fink H	"	
5034	"	Pickering J	"	
8494	"	Horley F	"	
10506	"	Potter H	"	
6872	Bugr	Bowden E	Died of wounds.	
898	Cpl	Goodspeed A	Wounded.	
8543	L/c	Letherby E	"	
7787	Cpl	Cloake B	"	
9427	Rfn	Earley G	"	
10045	"	Davey E	"	
10041	"	Stott W	"	
10241	"	Shorer E	"	
9169	L/c	Kenyon J	"	
8626	"	James C	"	
8791	Rfn	Timson S	"	
Captain C.J.T.R.Wingfield.			"	

Casualties 29th January 1915.

No.	Rank	Name	Nature of Casualty	Remarks
7191	Cpl	Coates A	Killed.	
7634	Rfn	Butlin	"	
xxxx	xxx	xxxxxxx	xxx	
Y1054	"	Hyslop A	Died of wounds.	
7795	"	Mills V	"	
9224	Rfn	Cox A	Wounded.	
8469	Bugr	Holder C	"	
10585	Rfn	Woodfield F	"	
2nd Lieutenant L.H.St A.King			"	

Casualties 30th January 1915.

No.	Rank	Name	Nature of Casualty	Remarks
3085	Sgt	Allen A	Killed.	
9136	Rfn	Devine M	"	
9633	"	Hudson W	Wounded.	
6856	Bug	Mayland F	"	
2834	Rfn	Wingrove F	"	
10452	"	Jones	"	
8422	"	Wickham	"	
7649	"	Couldwell J	"	
9338	"	Smith A	"	

To date:- Killed 27. Wounded Officers 5. Others 50.

A P P E N D I X   C.

Appendix "C"

REPORT ON THE ST ELOI SECTION OF TRENCHES.

The trenches of the first line are very deep in mud and water, some being above the waist, and cannot be naturally drained. These are, in my opinion, unfit for occupation in their present state.

Cover from fire is on the whole good but in many cases is not bullet proof. They are fairly well traversed and for the most part loopholed. Some trenches are provided with Dug-outs and some of these are dry and fit for occupation. Communication trenches are almost unuseable.

It is a matter of extreme difficulty and slowness to walk about in the trenches owing to the deep mud. Men have frequently to be pulled out and in a few cases have narrowly escaped drowning.

A considerable quantity of ammunition, stores, tools etc have been lost both in the trenches and in shell holes etc on the way to the trenches.

The state of the soil makes it extremely difficult to repair or improve the parapet especially as work on this can only be done at night.

The surrounding country is pitted with shell holes which greatly impede the bringing up of rations stores etc, by night. Consequent on the above state of affairs the men are after a period of twenty four hours in the trenches so exhausted that one journey out and in is all that they can manage and even that occupies the greater part of the night.

Telephonic communication is constantly interrupted by shell fire and in any case it is bad owing to the wet state of the ground which gets through any insulation. The wires have to be relaid nightly.

The Battalion headquarters were situated in a cellar which is insanitary owing to the presence of an old cesspool. It is also not bombproof.

The trenches of the company in support are generally speaking shrapnel proof, there is a great deal of water but the Dug-outs are dry in places.

REPORT

Rough sketch of the St. Eloi Section of trenches

Scale about 4" to 1m

[Signature] 12.1.16

WORK REQUIRED.

1. Render bullet proof everywhere.
2. Make dry standing room.
3. Improve communications.
4.   =   traverses.
5.   =   sanitation.
6.   "   DugNouts.
7. Make"new Battalion headquarters.

1. More tools. It might be possible to place sandbags and thicken the parapet by using the mud from the parado wherever it may not be required, as most of the first line trenches are not exposed to bombardment by high explosive shells.

2. It is very little use putting anything loose into the bottom of the trenches as things only disappear in the mud. Suggest putting ~~transverse~~ planks, corrugated ironsheeting etc on transverse beams, fixed into the sides of the trenches just above the level of the liquid mud. This might necessitate the raising of the parapet.

3. Communication trenches should be dug to the rear in view of next months moon. I do not see at present how troops could move up to the trenches in the light of a full moon without suffering considerably.

5. Latrine accomodation should be dug.

7. I suggest that a good bombproof be built some two hundred yards N.W. from the X roads in the village. It's present position is the centre of the area covered by the howitzer fire. This work would of course take time and should be carried out by sappers

8. There should be a little more in the way of entanglements

MATERIALS REQUIRED

Shovels, saws, beams, corrugated iron sheets etc, or any material suitable for "2", boarding etc for Dug-outs and a few axes and bill hooks.

Later when places are made for them more braziers.

A rough plan is attached.

80th Infantry Brigade.
27th Division.

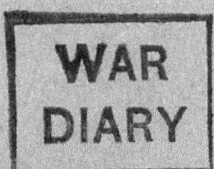

4th BATTN. THE KING'S ROYAL RIFLE CORPS.

F E B R U A R Y

1 9 1 5

Attached:
Appendix B.

4th Battalion The King's Royal Rifle Corps.

February 1915

1-2-15
(DICKEBUSCH)

Remained in billets

2-2-15

Remained in billets until 5.30 p.m. when the battalion marched to VOORMEZEELE to relieve 1st 4th Rifle Bde.

Army Form C. 2118.

WAR DIARY
or
INTELLIGENCE SUMMARY
(Erase heading not required.)

Hour, Date, Place	Summary of Events and Information	Remarks and references to Appendices
2-2-15. VOORMEZEELE	The Rifle Bde were relieved at 7.30.P.M. - C+D Coys went to ST ELOI to dig in rear of the trenches. C. Coy. had two casualties whilst digging both slightly wounded & knocked off digging at 11.20 p.m. D was relieved at 12.45 A.M. by B who continued to work until 4.30 a.m.	4/60th
3-2-15.	During the day the Battalion remained in VOORM:= ZEELE in close support. A few shells fell around but no damage was done. At dusk C Coy continued digging on the trenches of the previous night & worked on until midnight about 9.30 p.m. The remaining companies were employed carrying stores from KRUISSTRAATHOEK for R.E. purposes. D Coy then worked on the Crimean Trench until 12.30 A.M.	

Army Form C. 2118.

(29)

WAR DIARY
or
INTELLIGENCE SUMMARY
(Erase heading not required.)

Instructions regarding War Diaries and Intelligence Summaries are contained in F. S. Regs., Part II. and the Staff Manual respectively. Title pages will be prepared in manuscript.

Hour, Date, Place	Summary of Events and Information	Remarks and references to Appendices
4-2-15	where A. Coy. Relieved them. This coy worked on to 4.30.p.m. During the day the Battalion remained in VOORMEZEELE. Relief which should have been carried out by the Royal Irish was suspended until about 8.0 p.m. owing to a little activity on the front of the enemy on the front of the 28th Division. At 10.45. p.m. C. Coy went to KRUISSTRAATHOEK to carry rations to the P.P.C.L.I. in SHELLY FARM. At 11.20. P.M. It was reported that a trench on the left of the P.P.C.L.I. had been taken by the Germans & the Butts was ordered to proceed at once to Hedgerow 7.	4/60

1247 W 3209 200,000 (E) 8/14 J.B.C. & A. Forms/C. 2118/11.

WAR DIARY
or
INTELLIGENCE SUMMARY

Army Form C. 2118.

(30)

Hour, Date, Place	Summary of Events and Information	Remarks and references to Appendices
5-2-15	The P.P.C.L.I. at SHELLY FARM near ST ELOI. About 1.0 A.M. all being reported quiet 1st Battalion left ST ELOI & marched into huts about 1 mile N. of DICKEBUSCH. At 11.30 A.M. the march was continued to ZEVECOTON when the battalion went into huts. During the night of 5/4/6th 1st Batt'n were under orders to be ready to move at a moment's notice but nothing further occurred.	MD [illegible] 1/65th
5th — 9th Feb.	Rested in ZEVECOTON until 4.0 P.M. when 1st Battalion marched to the huts DICKEBUSCH.	
10-2-15 DICKEBUSCH	Left DICKEBUSCH at 5.30 P.M. and marched to ELZONVALLE BRASSERIE. From here the Battalion broke up and took over the	

Army Form C. 2118.

(31)

WAR DIARY
or
INTELLIGENCE SUMMARY
(Erase heading not required.)

Hour, Date, Place	Summary of Events and Information	Remarks and references to Appendices
RIGHT SECTION 27th DIV Trenches 11.2.15.	Trenches held by the Cameron Highlanders (who descended at Trenches 1 – 6 + S2 + S3 being part of the right section of the 27th Divisions area) Owing to an error in the numbering of the trenches the relief was not completed until almost midnight, as the K.S.L.I. on the right did not at first take on trench number 7 which had also been held by the Camerons. Headquarters remained at the ELZONVALE BRASSERIE. Casualties NIL.	Wm Gaffney Lt Col 4/60th
12.2.15. "Ditto."	Another uneventful day. A quiet day [the trenches in the neighbourhood of S3 + 4 were somewhat shelled but no damage was done.] Casualties 2 wounded (slightly) After dark the P.P.C.L.I. relieved the Battalion in the trenches the relief being complete by 10.45 P.M.	See Appendix "B"

Army Form C. 2118.

WAR DIARY
or
INTELLIGENCE SUMMARY
(Erase heading not required.)

(32)

Hour, Date, Place	Summary of Events and Information	Remarks and references to Appendices
12 - 2 - 15.	The Battalion marched back to DICKEBUSCH and went into the huts in support. Casualty 1 wounded.	see appendix "B" Wet Front Supplying
13 - 2 - 15.	Remained in huts in support all day. A cold miserable day.	
14 - 2 - 15.	Remained in huts another wet and cold day — Under orders to relieve PRCLI + RB + 8th into close support in Algarude ELZENWALLE and VIERSTRAAT but the were postponed at 6 p.m. owing to an attack on the ST ELOI trenches by the Germans who succeeded in capturing 19, 20, 21 & 22. An attack against the right of the 28th Division failed. About 7 pm the battalion got under arms + formed up on the road leading to DICKEBUSCH the K.S.L.I. being in front.	4/100th

Army Form C. 2118.

(33)

WAR DIARY
or
INTELLIGENCE SUMMARY

(Erase heading not required.)

Instructions regarding War Diaries and Intelligence Summaries are contained in F. S. Regs., Part II. and the Staff Manual respectively. Title pages will be prepared in manuscript.

Hour, Date, Place	Summary of Events and Information	Remarks and references to Appendices
	The 3rd Battalion had been ordered to ST ELOI. Orders were then received to move to a farm about 800 x SW of DICKEBUSCH church + this party went into billets for the night — The farm being on the VIERSTRAAT road — was a very crowded billet. At 5:30 A.M. A + B Coys under Major Bircham moved forward to the Second line of trenches behind VIERSTRAAT + continued work (digging etc) C + D Coys moved back to DICKEBUSCH at 6:15 a.m. and went into billets. A + B Coys got back from digging at about 10.30 a.m. The trenches where they were digging being violently shelled almost immediately after they had left.	4/66/a Submitted/approved
15 - 2 - 15.	Leaving DICKEBUSCH at 5:30 p.m. 1st Battalion relieved 1st P.P.C.L.I. in the right section of the trenches. The relief was carried out.	

Army Form C. 2118.

(34)

WAR DIARY
or
INTELLIGENCE SUMMARY
(Erase heading not required.)

Instructions regarding War Diaries and Intelligence Summaries are contained in F. S. Regs., Part II. and the Staff Manual respectively. Title pages will be prepared in manuscript.

Hour, Date, Place	Summary of Events and Information	Remarks and references to Appendices
15 - 2 - 15	Easily + without casualties.	
16 - 2 - 15	An uneventful day in the trenches casualties 1 wounded	Appendix B.
17 - 2 - 15	Little activity on the front of the enemy but one French was shelled. The battalion was relieved in the night of 17-18 by P.P.C.L.I. Casualties or H.O. Centre slightly wounded, other Ranks 2 killed & 7 wounded. [The Officer & 2 men were wounded after the relief when walking along the road.] The Battalion went into billets in DICKEBUSCH	1/60th Appendix B.
DICKEBUSCH 18.2.15	Remained in billets. No occurrence of note.	

Army Form C. 2118.

WAR DIARY
or
INTELLIGENCE SUMMARY
(Erase heading not required.)

(35)

Hour, Date, Place	Summary of Events and Information	Remarks and references to Appendices
DICKEBUSCH 19-2-15	Remained in DICKEBUSCH. At 7.15 P.M. moved to the relief of 4th R.B. sending A, B & D Coys to ELZONVALLE and C Coy to VIERSTRAAT.	
20-2-15 ELZONVALLE	An uneventful day — [Heavy gun and rifle fire from the direction of the Canal North of ST ELOI in the 28th Div area at about 4.30 p.m.]	4/60th
21-2-15	Another absolutely quiet day. A sharp burst of fire from the direction of ST ELOI at 6.0 a.m. — No shelling anywhere near ELZONVALLE. The Battalion was relieved at 8.0 p.m. at ELZONVALLE by the Leinster Regt & at VIERSTRAAT by the R.I. Fusiliers. The Battalion then marched back to ZEVECOTEN and went into huts.	

Army Form C. 2118.

36

WAR DIARY
or
INTELLIGENCE SUMMARY
(Erase heading not required.)

Hour, Date, Place	Summary of Events and Information	Remarks and references to Appendices
ZEVECOTON. 22-2-15 to 26-2-15	The Battalion remained in huts in ZEVECOTON during this period. The men were employed for the greater part of the time in making knife rest wire entanglements & laying down brushwood for paths between the huts.	
27-2-15. to DICKEBUSCH	Marched with the 3rd Batt⁵ from ZEVECOTON to DICKEBUSCH and on arrival went into billets (in and around the church. - Very uncomfortable -) moved down to ST ELOI arriving about 11.45 p.m	4/60th

Army Form C. 2118.

(37)

WAR DIARY
or
INTELLIGENCE SUMMARY

(Erase heading not required.)

Instructions regarding War Diaries and Intelligence Summaries are contained in F. S. Regs., Part II. and the Staff Manual respectively. Title pages will be prepared in manuscript.

4/65 d.

Hour, Date, Place	Summary of Events and Information	Remarks and references to Appendic
28-2-15.	The battalion dug until 4.15 a.m. making a new breastwork in rear of Trenches 19 – 21. Arrived back in DICKEBUSCH at about 6.30 A.M.	
	Continued work on the new breastwork starting digging at 7.16 P.M. & leaving off at 11.15 P.M. Returned to DICKEBUSCH about 12.45 A.M.	

A P P E N D I X   B.

Regl.No.	Rank	and Name		Nature of Casualty

Casualties 2nd February 1915.

| 7748 | Rfn | Clow | G. | Wounded. |
| 989 | " | Lucas | G. | " |

Casualties 11th and 12th February 1915.

12058	"	Hancock	C.	Wounded 11th.
8661	"	Collins	W.	"
8072	"	Beedell	W.	" 12th.

Casualties 16th and 17th February 1915.

9196	L/c	Evans	S.	Wounded 16th.
9585	Rfn	Hough	E.	" 17th. (Died 22nd)
8024	Cpl	Fielding	H.	Wounded 17th.
10584	Rfn	Woodley	T.	"
9158	L/c	Scotton	A.	"
10347	Rfn	Hirons	H.	"
10680	"	Cheshire	G.	"
10099	"	Hill	T.	Killed 17th.
3546	"	Atkins	G.	"
Lieut.		Curtis	H.O.	Wounded 17th.

Casualties 27th February 1915.

| 9909 | Rfn | Jones | A. | Wounded. |

Casualties 28th February 1915.

| 996 | " | Clarke | J. | Killed. |
| Y753 | " | Oldham | T. | Wounded. |

80th Infantry Brigade.
27th Division.

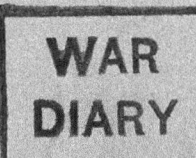

4th BATTN. THE KING'S ROYAL RIFLE CORPS.

M A R C H

1 9 1 5

Attached:

Appendices B
and C.

4th Battalion The King's Royal Rifle Corps.

March 1915

1-3-15	marched down to ST ELOI leaving DICKEBUSCH at 8.0 PM to carry out an attack on a German Trench. For details see appendix C.	Appendix "C"
2-3-15	Just before dawn the battalion was withdrawn into the new breastwork where it remained all day & moved back to DICKEBUSCH on the arrival of a party of	

Army Form C. 2118.

(30)

WAR DIARY
or
INTELLIGENCE SUMMARY
(Erase heading not required.)

Instructions regarding War Diaries and Intelligence Summaries are contained in F.S. Regs., Part II. and the Staff Manual respectively. Title pages will be prepared in manuscript.

Hour, Date, Place	Summary of Events and Information	Remarks and references to Appendices
3-3-15	PPCLI. to dig in new trench in rear of 21. Did not get back to DICKEBUSCH until about 1.0 a.m	
3-3-15	Starting from DICKEBUSCH at 5.45 PM 1st Battalion relieved the 3rd Battalion in the left ST ELOI Section. Major Widdrington - C.O. was unfortunately hit through the shoulder when going round the trenches	4/6 OR See Casualty List
4-3-15	Enemy shelled ST ELOI with howitzers for about two hours very heavily - Fortunately their fire was confined to an occupied area and this particular fire caused no casualties.	See Casualty List

1247 W 8299 200,000 (E) 8/14 J.B.C. & A. Forms/C. 2118/11.

Army Form C. 2118.

(39)

WAR DIARY
or
INTELLIGENCE SUMMARY
(Erase heading not required.)

Instructions regarding War Diaries and Intelligence Summaries are contained in F. S. Regs., Part II. and the Staff Manual respectively. Title pages will be prepared in manuscript.

Hour, Date, Place	Summary of Events and Information	Remarks and references to Appendices
ST. ELOI 5-3-15.	A very quiet day — Practically no shelling — relieved by 3rd Battn at night. This relief was somewhat delayed by the relief for 21 trench — Completed at 11.45 P.M.	Selmony Copyright
DICKEBUSCH 6-3-15	Remained in Support	
7-3-15	Starting from DICKEBUSCH at 6 P.M. relieved 3rd Battn. Relief complete by 9.30 p.m. without Casualties	
8-3-15	A quiet day practically no shelling — a few Casualties See appendix	

Army Form C. 2118.

(4D)

WAR DIARY
or
INTELLIGENCE SUMMARY
(Erase heading not required.)

Instructions regarding War Diaries and Intelligence Summaries are contained in F.S. Regs, Part II. and the Staff Manual respectively. Title pages will be prepared in manuscript.

Hour, Date, Place	Summary of Events and Information	Remarks and references to Appendices
9.3.15 ST ELOI	The enemy's trenches before ST ELOI were shelled all day — The enemy replied a little but did little damage (see 80th IB. Op order 24) After dark the Battalion was relieved by the 3rd Batⁿ. There was only one casualty during the period. midnight 8th = 9th to relief being completed	Stilmon/ Cpt/Adjt
10.3.15 DICKEBUSCH	Remained in Support	

Army Form C. 2118.

(41)

WAR DIARY
or
INTELLIGENCE SUMMARY

(Erase heading not required.)

Instructions regarding War Diaries and Intelligence Summaries are contained in F. S. Regs., Part II. and the Staff Manual respectively. Title pages will be prepared in manuscript.

Hour, Date, Place	Summary of Events and Information	Remarks and references to Appendices
11-3-15	Remained in support until relieved after dusk by 1st Irish Brigade. (82nd) when 1st Battalion marched to ZEVECOTEN and went into huts.	
12-3-15 ZEVECOTEN	Remained in reserve - Four Officers joined. Capt H. W. M. Walton taking on Command of the Battalion.	
13-3-15 ZEVECOTEN	In Reserve.	

Army Form C. 2118.

(42)

WAR DIARY
or
INTELLIGENCE SUMMARY
(Erase heading not required.)

Instructions regarding War Diaries and Intelligence Summaries are contained in F.S. Regs., Part II. and the Staff Manual respectively. Title pages will be prepared in manuscript.

Hour, Date, Place	Summary of Events and Information	Remarks and references to Appendices
14 – 3 – 15 ZEVECOTEN	In Reserve –	
5.20 pm	Heavy artillery fire heard from 1st division of DICKEBUSCH.	
6.0 pm	Orders Received to Stand ready to move.	
6.40 pm	" " move to DICKEBUSCH.	
7.0 pm	Marched for DICKEBUSCH – On arrival at ½ Battalion was ordered to continue march to VOORMEZEELE and then went to G.O.C. 82nd Bde. Packs were taken off & Options & some men Dixie – BUSCH. The Battalion then proceeded to the edge of trenches	

Army Form C. 2118.

43

WAR DIARY
or
INTELLIGENCE SUMMARY
(Erase heading not required.)

Hour, Date, Place	Summary of Events and Information	Remarks and references to Appendices
Midnight 14th–15th	between KRUISSTRAATHOEK and VOORMEZEELE. Ordered to march to the sunken road situated between SHELLEY FARM and ST ELOI. Information had been received by this time that Hammond and a certain number of trenches before ST ELOI had been captured by the Enemy.	
15.3.15. 2. A.M.	After being greatly delayed by troops in and near VOORMEZEELE the head of the battalion was just crossing the YPRES road about 500 yds N of ST ELOI in a very strung out formation. At this moment the part of the 82nd Bde. falling back	

WAR DIARY or INTELLIGENCE SUMMARY

Army Form C. 2118.
(45)

Hour, Date, Place	Summary of Events and Information	Remarks and references to Appendices
	It was then decided to withdraw in the direction of YOORMEZEELE with a view to reforming the Bn. Captain Stewart had in the meantime been reforming that part of the battalion which had been cut off from the head of the column and eventually the whole battalion was once more assembled immediately south of ENVERIN YOORMEZEELE. and under the C.O. of the 80th T.Bn's.	
4.30 a.m.	moved in to take H.Q. of 18th Bde between ST ELOI. Orders were received to occupy trenches S.11.d.12. —	
	It was not immediately south of YOORMEZEELE, nore to commence the work demand of the Brigade at dayn	
6.30 a.m.	The Brigade having withdrawn intermediate formed meant was held at DIKKE BOSCH.	

Army Form C. 2118.

(46)

WAR DIARY
or
INTELLIGENCE SUMMARY
(Erase heading not required.)

Instructions regarding War Diaries and Intelligence Summaries are contained in F. S. Regs, Part II. and the Staff Manual respectively. Title pages will be prepared in manuscript.

Hour, Date, Place	Summary of Events and Information	Remarks and references to Appendices
16-3-15. 7.15 P.M.	A Coy made up to 100 rifles took over the trench work from the Royal Irish Fusiliers. The night being still in the forenoon of the Schnaeus the situation seemed critical. The work of bending look No 1 got up one looking was started with a view to opening to work from outside the front. The remainder of the battalion remained in Diche.	
17-3-15	BUSCH - Draft of 3 officers and 60 NCOs R/m arrived. B Coy made up to 120 (ones) 2 draft for A Coy + also 10th over. 2nd draft R-3 from 10 N.S.L.I. Captain James was unfortunately killed while continuing	

Army Form C. 2118.

WAR DIARY
or
INTELLIGENCE SUMMARY
(Erase heading not required.)

Instructions regarding War Diaries and Intelligence Summaries are contained in F.S. Regs., Part II. and the Staff Manual respectively. Title pages will be prepared in manuscript.

Hour, Date, Place	Summary of Events and Information	Remarks and references to Appendices
18-3-15	to work on the breastwork. — 3 officers (joined)	Military Appendix
	C Coy made up relieved the Breastwork & returned & continued to work on the Breastwork	
19-3-15	A Coy made up to strength again relieved the breastwork firstly & relieved.	
20-3-15	B Coy relieved A Coy. The same work being carried on	
21-3-15	C Coy relieved B. and continued the work.	

Army Form C. 2118.

WAR DIARY
or
INTELLIGENCE SUMMARY
(Erase heading not required.)

Hour, Date, Place	Summary of Events and Information	Remarks and references to Appendices
ST ELOI		
22-3-15	Prolonging the Throw back flank. A Coy relieved B in the saurs work.	
23-3-15	B + C Coys. relieved the Breastwork & redoubt as usual	
24-3-15	Royal Fusiliers 85th Bde. took over the breastwork & redoubt from the battalion. The Garrison now being 130 for the Breastwork + 20 and a machine gun for the redoubt. The battalion then marched to billets between RENINGHELST and POPERINGHE.	Cas. O₉ʳ - 24" K 1 + 10 W 13.

Army Form C. 2118.

1st K R R C
49

WAR DIARY
or
INTELLIGENCE SUMMARY
(Erase heading not required.)

Hour, Date, Place	Summary of Events and Information	Remarks and references to Appendices
near POPERINGHE 25-3-15	The Reinforced Companies arrived in billets about 4.30 a.m. The battalion being now in rest the time was devoted to training, musketry, etc. On 31-3-15. a party of 300 was sent up to DICKIEBUSCH to dig on the G.H.Q line of trenches returning at 2.20 a.m. 1-4-15 On 29-3-15 a draft of 77 N.C.O. & Men arrived mostly old 4th & 2nd R⁵ men	2nd in offig Major

Instructions regarding War Diaries and Intelligence Summaries are contained in F. S. Regs., Part II. and the Staff Manual respectively. Title pages will be prepared in manuscript.

APPENDIX B.

Regl.No.	Rank	Name		Nature of casualty

Casualties 1st and 2nd March contd.
Wounded.

Regl.No.	Rank	Name			Regl.No.	Rank	Name	
9613	Rfn	Cooper	T.		7005	Rfn	Carter	H.
9876	"	Palmer	F.		7879	Bgr	Day	W.
9989	"	Clarke	E.		8854	Rfn	Dick	R.
223	"	Carroll	P.		7150	"	Edwards	J.
1251	"	Raynor	J.		10123	"	Elliott	J.
7557	"	Reed	G.		8510	"	Elvins	W.
Y1662	"	Kirkman	J.		9715	"	Haley	T.
3545	"	Stewart	J.		11367	"	Harrodd	J.
470	"	Stark	S.		7808	"	Hill	J.
9304	"	Ridley	A.		10091	L/c	Hunt	R.
10399	"	Newton	A.		7332	Rfn	Jennings	A.
3307	"	Atkins	B.		10580	"	Poulton	J.
9718	"	Grace	C.		8000	L/c	Scivier	W.
8056	"	Shepherd	W.		9723	Rfn	Hutchins	C.
9338	"	Smith	A.		11007	"	Blackman	G.
8438	"	Townsend	R.		12115	"	Carson	A.
10500	"	Witt	H.		Y 499	"	Collins	R.
7792	"	Cleaver	G.		6258	"	Lishman	W.
Y 349	"	Parker	G.					

Missing.

Regl.No.	Rank	Name			Regl.No.	Rank	Name	
Captain		Poe	C.V.L.		Captain		Lagden	R.O.
Lieut.		Eden Hon.	W.A.M.		1351	Rfn	French	E.
10826	Rfn	English	C.		6271	Cpl	Griffiths	F.
9850	L/c	Beech	C.		7855	Rfn	Hogg	G.
8919	"	Butt	F.		10174	L/c	Ingram	W.
9141	"	Seed	W.		8553	Rfn	Lawlor	J.
8038	Rfn	Billingham	G.		9916	"	Lock	A.
9506	"	Burden	R.		9198	"	Marr	E.
9545	"	Clarke	J.		4988	"	Morgan	A.
7816	"	Eason	A.		10049	"	Sell	E.
9196	L/c	Evans	S.		7916	"	Straker	J.
11796	Rfn	Ewen	J.		7932	L/c	Warner	E.
8971	L/c	Foreman	E.		4411	Rfn	Turner	W.
Y1175	Rfn	Magra	W.		7077	"	Tyson	T.
A 236	"	Moseley	A.		152	"	Weller	H.
11470	L/c	Palmer	T.		10797	"	Winstone	T.
10599	Rfn	Potter	H.					

Casualties 3rd March 1915.

Regl.No.	Rank	Name		Nature
2100	C.S.M.	Griffin	G.	Killed.
11249	Rfn	Turner	A.	"
R5982	"	Keyser	A.	Wounded.
7214	"	Hinson	J.	"

Casualties 4th March 1915.

Regl.No.	Rank	Name		Nature
Major		Widdrington	B.F.	Wounded.
2132	Rfn	Ratcliffe	E.	Killed.
Y615	"	Kemp	J.	Wounded.
9146	"	Roan	R.	Wounded.

Casualties 5th March 1915.

Regl.No.	Rank	Name		Nature
7728	Cpl	Goody	J.	Killed.
Lieut.		Curtis	H.O.	Wounded.
Lieut.		Hill	V.B.	"
7748	Rfn	Clow	G.	"
6975	"	Freeman	C.	"
10421	"	Webb	R.	"

Casualties 8th and 9th March 1915.

Regl.No.	Rank	Name		Nature
Lieut.		Curtis	H.O.	Wounded 8th.

```
Regl.No.   Rank and Name.              Nature of casualty.
```

Casualties 8th and 9th March contd.

Regl.No.	Rank	Name		Nature
10019	Rfn	Callant	T.	Killed. 8th.
7743	L/c	Peace	A.	Wounded 8th.
8673	Bgr	Jones	E.	"
9903	Rfn	Forey	J.	"
5169	"	Bolton	E.	"
9004	L/c	Prescott	J.	"
7794	Rfn	Minns	A.	"
9872	"	Seager	F.	" 9th.

Casualty 7th March 1915.

10417 A/Cpl Nelson R.   Died of wounds, accidental, self inflicted.

Casualties 1st and 2nd March 1915.

Regl.No.	Rank	Name		Nature
8430	L/c	Griffiths	E.	Killed.
172	C.S.M.	Hinds	A.	"
7919	Sgt	Newham	R.	"
8436	Rfn	Wagg	J.	"
10465	"	Rudder	A.	"
3691	"	Tomkins	A.	"
9721	"	Pearsall	A.	"
10840	"	Ault	G.	"
7706	"	Phipps	J.	"
8020	Sgt	Poole	C.	"
1428	"	Butler	H.	"
6628	"	Oram	G.	"
8699	"	Collins	G.	"
5576	Cpl	Hooker	G.	"
6171	=	Mockford	A.	"
10819	Rfn	Wells	J.	"

Wounded.

Regl.No.	Rank	Name		Regl.No.	Rank	Name	
Major		Bircham	H.F.W.	Lieut.		Barker	E.H.
8600	Cpl	Parr	G.	5047	Rfn	Dibbling	T.
8019	L/c	Hawkins	A.	10865	L/c	Surridge	G.
9011	Rfn	Barringer	H.	11952	"	Llewellyn	G.
Y1201	"	Barron	F.	1005	"	Francis	E.
Y 647	"	Broome	J.	8057	"	Cook	E.
8041	"	Whitehouse	F.	9029	Rfn	Whittaker	R.
Y 818	"	Round	A.	7146	"	Cheshire	H.
8542	"	Brothers	C.	8500	Sgt	Beards	W.
9979	"	Hill	H.	7779	L/c	Ayres	H.
1215	"	Astley	W.	8578	Cpl	Prax	J.
10235	"	Harwood	E.	10156	Rfn	Applebee	J.
2854	"	Lindley	G.	8772	L/c	Buckley	J.

Appendix "B"

Regl.No.	Rank	and Name.		Nature of Casualty.

Casualties 14th - 15th March 1915.

3044	S.M.	Brasier	T.	Wounded 14th.
6574	Sgt	O'Connor	T.	"
Y1188	Rfn	Smith	H.	"
6772	"	Litherland	H.	"
1147	"	Skeets	T.	"
Y1823	"	Turner	H.	"
988	"	Hesson	G.	" 15th accident.

Casualties 17.3.15.

12034	"	Haggar	T.	Wounded.
9330	"	Greenwood	B.	"
Captain		James	E.S.P.K.	Killed.
5775	L/c	Laws	M.	Wounded, died 18th.

Casualties 18.3.1915.

7233	Sgt	Hindle	J.	Killed.
10034	Rfn	Anderson	W.	"
8511	"	Boston	G.	Wounded. (since dead)
4406	"	Flaxington	G.	" "

Casualty 19.3.1915.

| 884 | " | Dilgert | T. | Killed. |

Casualties 19-20.3.1915.

2429	Sgt	Coxon	G.	Wounded 19th.
423	Rfn	Riddle	W.	" 20th.
2071	"	Jackson	J.	" " (since dead)
5795	"	Adams	N.	" "

Casualty 21.3.15.

| 7137 | " | Bradford | A. | Wounded, since dead. |

Casualty 22.3.15.

| 5778 | " | Earl | T. | Killed. |

Further Casualties 15th March 1915.

| 982 | L/c | Harris | G. | Wounded, since dead. |
| 10094 | Rfn | Bell | B. | Wounded. |

| 8415 | Rfn | H Hosker. | | Wounded 23.3.15. |

A P P E N D I X C.

Appendix "C"

4th Battalion The King's Royal Rifle Corps.

Report

On the Operations near ST ELOI on the night of 1st – 2nd March 1915.

The Battalion left DICKEBUSCH at 8.0 P.M and marched direct to the "new Breastwork" in rear of Trenches 19 – 21 where the companies were formed up in the following order from right to left. A, C, B, D.

The battalion remained in this position until the relief of the trenches then held by the P.P.C.L.I had been duly carried out by the 3rd Batt= K.R.R.C. The Commanding Officer + company commanders then went forward to a point in rear of 21 to reconnoitre the line of advance.

Plan of Action

The line of advance was to be via the routes marked in red on the attached plan. The intention being to enter the German trench on the left of 21 + carry the whole length up to the OOSTAVERNE road in one rush.

The leading company, D, under Captain C.V.L. Poë was to carry out this operation, passing straight on and out at the road near the mound, reassembling behind the right of the "new Breastwork".

Meanwhile "B" Coy under Maj Bircham and "C" Coy under Capt. Hunter were to follow on in rear of "D" & occupy the trench.

These two companies had shovels and sandbags, and had orders to start work immediately making the captured trench capable of being used as a fire trench facing the main German line.

"A" Coy under Lt A.E. Lawrence was to move to the left end of the breastwork & remain in reserve.

The attacking column was to have its head resting in 21, two platoons being closed up for this purpose. The signal to advance was to be the opening of fire by the Artillery.

Action.

By 12.10.a.m. the head of the leading company was into 21 and had started closing up. At 12.15.a.m. the Artillery were requested to open fire at 12.30 AM by which hour it was considered that all would be ready. This message was acknowledged.

At 12.30 precisely the Guns opened a very accurate fire and the leading platoon under Lt The Hon W.A.M. Eden rushed forward & got into the end of the enemy's trench. The enemy apparently ran at once & the occupants of 21 under Captain Sir G. Beaumont 3rd Bn K.R.R.C. report having killed a few as they fled across the open.

From this moment accurate information as to what happened at the head of the column is hard to obtain. The Column still lead by Captain C.V.L. Poë, Lt Eden & Lt Vivian K.S.LI. with a few bomb-throwers, pushed on up to the Barricade at X.

Just in front of this was a wire entanglement described as a "Gate" & between this and the Barricade three Germans were caught & killed.

From what evidence can be obtained part of the attacking party then bore right headed down the trench marked "Z" & eventually came out past the right of 21. Captains Poë & Raglan lead straight on towards the barricade.

By this time the Barricade was heavily manned by

by Germans. who shot & bombed down the last stretch of Trench.

Captains Poë & Lagden then endeavoured to get out of the Trench to the German rear with a view to getting round behind the Barricade.

Rifle & machine Gun fire however from the main German Trench so swept the open zone that any man standing up was immediately hit.

Captain Poë was hit here at least twice & it is I fear beyond doubt that he was killed.

From all accounts his last order to his men was to get back into the trench he having apparently realised that it was futile to endeavour to get up in the open. Accounts as to what happened to Lieut Edson vary but it is stated that he was the first man up to the barricade & succeeded in getting out of the trench on the German side & was last seen running as if endeavouring to get round the Barricade.

All accounts are unanimous as to his having, like Captain Poë, lead his men to the very end with the utmost gallantry.

The stretch of Trench nearest the barricade was now

full of killed and wounded the whole of "D" company having been absorbed.

At this point Maj Bircham with the head of "B" Coy arrived at the bend at point "B". A few men of "D" Coy were left in front of him & were unable to move forward owing to the trench being full of dead and wounded & to the fact that the moment that a man showed his head round the corner he came under fire from the Barricade, which from all accounts appears to have been a kind of miniature fort wired all round & loopholed.

At this point I came up with Maj Bircham & seeing the situation as shown above I ordered him to start preparing the trench for defence. & then went to ST ELOI to report on the Telephone to the G.O.C 80TH INF BDE. At the same time I ordered "C" Coy who were lying in the open to withdraw to near SHELLY FARM.

In accordance with instructions from G.O.C. the trench was handed over to 3rd Bn K.R.R.C at that time occupying 21.

The enemy's fire had considerably slackened over the General area but a few more casualties occurred during the withdrawal.

Major Bircham who throughout had behaved with great coolness was unfortunately hit when leaving the trench in rear of his company.

By the time the last man had withdrawn behind the breastwork it was about 5.45. a.m. & getting light

The Battalion remained behind the "new Breast-Work" during daylight of 2nd March & withdrew at night when the 3rd Batt'n had safely started work on the New trench in rear of 21.

I attribute failure to capture more of the German trench to the following causes:—

(i) That the enemy were in every way prepared for the attack having taken warning by their previous experience.

(ii) That, once the surprise was over, the barricade was virtually impregnable under the combined fire of the enemy from it & the main position in rear.

(iii) That the depth of the enemy's trench was such

that sufficient men could not get out at one time to assault the barricade.

(IV) That almost immediately the operations began the moon came out full & the night remained clear.

Casualties

Officers :- Major H.F.W. Bircham ⎫ Wounded
Lieut E.H. Barker ⎭

Capt. C.V.L. Poë ⎫
" R.O. Lagden ⎬ missing
Lieut. The Hon. W.A.M. Eden ⎭

Rank & File   16 Killed
              61 Wounded
              30 Missing (many feared killed).

In the Field

3-3-15.

B.A. Heddington Major.
The Kings Royal Rifle Corps.
Commanding 4th Battalion.

Rough Sketch to Illustrate Operations of 1st – 2nd March 1914.

(not to scale)

Q — X about 60 yds
P — Q " 15 "

Main German Trench.

German Trench

To Oostaverne

To Wytschaete

mound

ST ELOI.

To YPRES

To VOORMEZEELE

19
19a
20
21
22
New Breastwork

Sd/ Maurice Cope
Lieut Maurice Cope Capt
2.3.15.

Rough Plan of The German Trench.

Plan

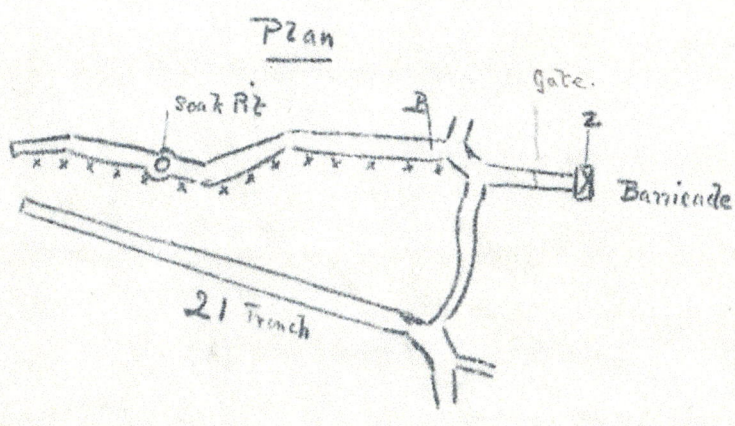

Section of Average Part of Trench

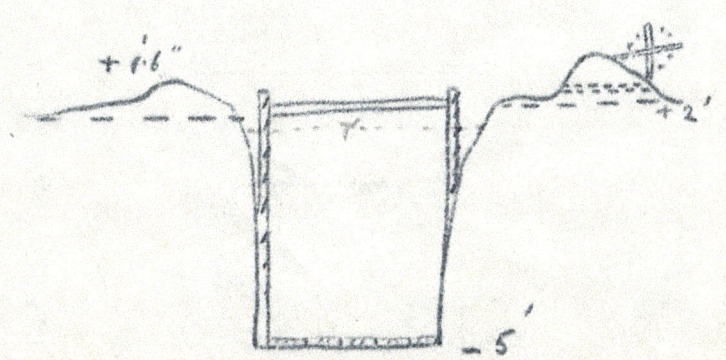

Section of Trench at Sump Pit

H. Consmy Capt.
The King's Royal Rifle Corps.
3. 3. 15.

80th Infantry Brigade.
27th Division.

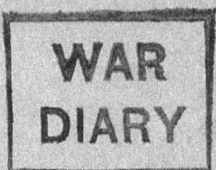

4th BATTN. THE KING'S ROYAL RIFLE CORPS.

A P R I L

1 9 1 5

Attached:
    Casualty List.

4th Battn. The King's Royal Rifle Corps.

April 1915

4-4-15	On 2-4-15 a party of 150 were sent to work on the line of the trenches near DICKEBUSCH.

Army Form C. 2118.

WAR DIARY
or
INTELLIGENCE SUMMARY
(Erase heading not required.)

Hour, Date, Place	Summary of Events and Information	Remarks and references to Appendices
5-4-15.	Marched at 8.45 a.m. to billets immediately west of VLAMERTINGHE arriving at 10.45 a.m.	
6th-8th-4-15.	Remained in VLAMERTINGHE. A draft of 100 other ranks including a detachment of 41 from FIJI arrived. On 8th a number of Officers went to visit the new section of trenches then held by K.S.L.I.	
9-4-15.	Marched at 4 p.m. to YPRES Barracks and rested there until 8 p.m. when the Battalion paraded and marched to the trenches taking on from the K.S.L.I. These trenches though not first class were very pleasant after those at ST ELOI.	

WAR DIARY or **INTELLIGENCE SUMMARY**

Army Form C. 2118.

(Erase heading not required.)

Instructions regarding War Diaries and Intelligence Summaries are contained in F. S. Regs., Part II. and the Staff Manual respectively. Title pages will be prepared in manuscript.

Hour, Date, Place	Summary of Events and Information	Remarks and references to Appendices
10 – 4 – 15.	An uneventful day – Quiet on both sides	
11 – 4 – 15.	Another quiet day – relieved by K.S.L.I. getting back to YPRES about 2.30 A.M. 12-4-15.	
12th + 13th - 4 - 15	Remained in YPRES – Quiet on both days	
14 – 4 – 15	Marched to trenches starting 7.30 p.m. took over from K.S.L.I.	
15 – 4 – 15.	A quiet day except for a little shelling near NOYNNE BOSCHEN WOOD	

Army Form C. 2118.

WAR DIARY
or
INTELLIGENCE SUMMARY

(Erase heading not required.)

Instructions regarding War Diaries and Intelligence Summaries are contained in F. S. Regs., Part II. and the Staff Manual respectively. Title pages will be prepared in manuscript.

Hour, Date, Place	Summary of Events and Information	Remarks and references to Appendices
16-4-15	Fairly quiet - some shelling of VERBEEK FARM / a few shots going near 75 French - one J blew in a portion of the parapet.	
17-4-15	A quiet day - Owing to an enterprise taking place a little way South of the battalion was not relieved until 1 A.M. 18-4-15	
18-4-15 } 19-4-15 }	On relief marched to BELLEWAARDE near HOOGE + went into dug out. Remained here in comparative peace until 20-4-15. A good deal of Artillery fire on both sides but no	

Army Form C. 2118.

(53)

WAR DIARY
or
INTELLIGENCE SUMMARY

(Erase heading not required.)

Hour, Date, Place	Summary of Events and Information	Remarks and references to Appendices
	Shells pitched actually in the dug-out area	
	On 19-4-15 a draft of 68 arrived with Captain C.J.T.R Winyfield now recovered from wounds	
20-4-15.	About 5.45 P.M. the enemy opened a very heavy fire of shrapnel on the trenches and shortly was being brought from the trenches which were opposite the [illegible] north of BELLEWAARDE LAKE [illegible] The fuses shells falling [illegible] [illegible] a [illegible] [illegible] [illegible] The fire died out & military [illegible] The [illegible] [illegible] ran and appeared to have been [illegible] In operation by the neighbourhood of WR 6c. Fumes were very [illegible]	
10.30 P.M.	The 3rd Battalion the East [illegible] BELLEWAARDE WOOD to relieve the K.R.R.C. in the trenches near BOS. VEN WOOD	

Army Form C. 2118.

WAR DIARY
or
INTELLIGENCE SUMMARY

(Erase heading not required.)

Instructions regarding War Diaries and Intelligence Summaries are contained in F. S. Regs., Part II. and the Staff Manual respectively. Title pages will be prepared in manuscript.

Hour, Date, Place	Summary of Events and Information	Remarks and references to Appendices
21-4-15	A very quiet day. Only a little shelling of the trenches and a few into BOESINGHE WOOD	
22-4-15	Another quiet day — usual shelling of KORTEKEER and troops & the batteries from YELDHOEK and BOESINGHE	
23-4-15	Heavy firing in the direction of ST JULIEN and PILKEM. The sound appeared to come from (French) [guns?] There was also a great deal of shelling all round the Salient. The enemy again using gas.	
24-4-15	The battle went home. Continued all day. We heard enemy artillery was a great [?] to front to Salient. In our front the enemy [?] [?] [?] right of the line. The [?] [?] firing all day & afterwards we saw of enemy a division in this direction	
7.30 A.M. 25-4-15 BOESCHEN WOOD	Shelled. Also saw working parties etc.	

1247 W 3299 200,000 (E) 8/14 J.B.C. & A. Forms/C. 2118/11.

WAR DIARY or INTELLIGENCE SUMMARY

Army Form C. 2118.

Hour, Date, Place	Summary of Events and Information	Remarks and references to Appendices
26 – 4 – 15	An exceptionally quiet night which led us to suppose that the enemy was changing their troops in the front line + or moving troops with a view to attack. At 4.10 a.m. Battalion opened heavy fire on our finishing work BOSCHEN WOOD. One shell H.E. howitzer shrapnel bursting just over the trenches killed four and wounded six. At 11.15 a.m. the Germans were seen not infantry another shell hitting from Bn't or many men. One but which were firing got left several for the most part to be denoted on KESTHOFR and no ground kept. Again at 10.10 P.M. the above action was simultaneously shelled.	(26/4) Note – Knocked in wrong words in trench here

Army Form C. 2118.

WAR DIARY
or
INTELLIGENCE SUMMARY

(Erase heading not required.)

Instructions regarding War Diaries and Intelligence Summaries are contained in F.S. Regs., Part II. and the Staff Manual respectively. Title pages will be prepared in manuscript.

Hour, Date, Place	Summary of Events and Information	Remarks and references to Appendices

21–4–15

A comparatively quiet day as regard to rifle fire in our lines in front of Kemmel. About 2 p.m. the enemy started shell about 20 minutes. Enemy fire continued to 9 p.m. in the neighbourhood.

22–4–15

2 Infantry Bgd on our right relieved & it is so in action.

A vehement fire was coming fairly heavy f.c. about 9.0 minutes. The enemy were reported at 6.30 p.m. to have broken our line & succeeded in getting into [?]

At 8.30 p.m. a little intense fire was observed to the [?] Ypres Road on right. The day continued fairly quiet up to [?] when heavy bombardment from our artillery & M.G. & rifle [?] broke in [?] from out of the trenches & an implement

F. Kerr

Army Form C. 2118.

4 ITRR

WAR DIARY
or
INTELLIGENCE SUMMARY

(Erase heading not required.)

Instructions regarding War Diaries and Intelligence Summaries are contained in F. S. Regs., Part II. and the Staff Manual respectively. Title pages will be prepared in manuscript.

Hour, Date, Place	Summary of Events and Information	Remarks and references to Appendices
29th (Continued)	7 – 8 p.m. a battery of Heavy Howitzers fired 60–80 rounds at the aid dumping ground just N of BOESCHEN WOOD from almost due east.	
30 – 4 – 15	Shortly after daylight kings being made hard at N.W. direction somewhere on the YSER canal – remained surroundings were throughout a day comparatively quiet	

CASUALTY LIST.

10116	L/c	W Eves.	Wounded 10.4.15.
7186	Rfn	W Yearby.	"
Y1860	"	B Bradley.	"
7125	Sgt	V Gray.	Wounded 11.4.15.
R9920	Rfn	B Macauly.	"
R10185	"	D Thompson.	"
9237	"	C Youngman.	"
6714	"	E Browning.	Wounded 16.4.15.
Y505	"	F Wicks.	Wounded 15.4.15.
Y515	"	E Bollen.	Wounded 16.4.15.
R987	A/c	W Reid.	"
11729	Rfn	H Parker.	Wounded 17.4.15.
8778	L/c	G Lucas.	Wounded 18.4.15.
9640	C.Q.M.S.	Shone.	"
3080	Sgt	W Hetherington.	"
8710	L/c	D Deighton.	Killed 20.4.15.
R5113	Rfn	A Budd.	"
R3599	"	J Wood.	"
10458	L/c	A Wood.	"
11772	Rfn	J Holmes.	Wounded "
8575	"	W Smith.	Wounded 22.4.15.

Casualties 23.4.15.

Killed.
Y801 " J Donovan.
R4115 " A Howarth.   827 Rfn E Edwards.   Y962 Rfn J Mansfield.
8395 L/S N Wilson.   R10204 " V Abrahams.   11562 " R Fowler.
R1204 Rfn C Burgess.   R8889 A/c M Reddie.   R9926 " D O'Mahoney.
R10202 L/C C Niven.   Capt.C.J.T.R.Wingfield.   Lieut.J.B.Ellis.

Casualties 24.4.15.

Killed. Y681 Rfn E Chignall.   12064 Rfn G Kilham.   10902 O.Underwood.
Y406 Rfn H Grace.   Y 318 Rfn W Green.
Wounded. 9282 Sgt C Macdonald.   9967 Rfn B Coleman.   4974 R Foster.
9947 Rfn J Austin.   1033 Rfn Fallowfield.

Casualties 25.4.15.

Killed. R9330 Rfn Neville.   10495 Rfn Gobey.   A 544 Rfn A Kemp.
Wounded. 11407 Rfn Seaman.   8771 Rfn Meacham.   10108 Rfn Gale.   7999 Rfn W Terry.   Y1191 Rfn Bushell.   10448 Rfn Hancock.   10168 Rfn James.
2303 Rfn Hague.

Casualties 26.4.15.

Killed. 3295 Sgt Coles.   R10102 A/c Williams.   Y1053 Rfn Davis.   10060 Rfn O'Brien.   6631 Rfn H Enderby.   Y1695 Rfn Taylor.   7729 Bgr F Munro.
Wounded. 9730 A/c R Jobes.   8531 Cpl T Duffy.   7703 Rfn S Woods.   Y1348 Rfn Argent.   Y511 Rfn Whitehouse.   9236 Rfn W Brindle.   12260 Rfn Russell T.
2834 Rfn Wingrove F.   10179 Rfn Walker.   7845 Sgt G Horne.   9782 Cpl J Brannigan.   9940 A/c G Kirby.   10114 L/c W Burgess.   9934 L/c Ford.   1760 Rfn Coombes.   10453 Rfn Browning.   4848 Rfn Harrison.   10406 Rfn Brockman.
4166 Rfn Davis.   Y611 Rfn Lowe.   6105 Rfn W Sheehy.   10797 Rfn Bennett.
4635 Rfn Lunn.   8198 Rfn Nichols.   Y1719 Rfn B Royal.   10190 Rfn Grey.
10175 Rfn Simmons.   10258 Rfn Clarke.   1032 Rfn Dale.   5895 Rfn Fox.
Y434 Rfn Thomas.   2nd Lieut.T.A.Butcher.

Casualties 27.4.15.

Wounded. 9774 Rfn W Hawkes.   11688 Rfn G Smith.   5199 Rfn Hodgkins.

Casualties 28.4.15.

Killed. 8819 Cpl R Mayell.
Wounded. 772 Rfn A Shelley.   8046 Rfn F Cooling.   8149 Rfn W Farley.   7588 Bdm C Southgate.   R11627 Rfn Hendrick E.   6053 Rfn F Howard.   9195 Rfn C Etherington.   10169 Rfn C James.   R10471 Rfn E Tagg.

6936	Bdm	A McInnis.	Killed 29.4.15.
9892	Rfn	W Harvey.	"
Y1180	L/c	A Gwynne.	Wounded 30.4.15.

80th Infantry Brigade.
27th Division.

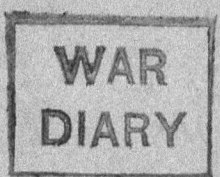

4th BATTN. THE KING'S ROYAL RIFLE CORPS.

M A Y

1 9 1 5

Attached:
Casualty List.

4th Battalion The King's Royal Rifle Corps.

May 1915

1-15-15		Again a very quiet day [?] 2.10 a.m. no 3 Coy came + BOSCHEN WOOD M.G. detail of field partol.
2-5-15		Austr. until 5.15 P.M. when enemy being broken out on the direction of ST JULIAN on 50 N. to S.W. of us. Salient. This was taken up, but after two approaches by Hampshires appeared no, which kept up a heavy cannonade fire. But on our front + rules the salient. At 6.50 P.M. the fire began to slacken all round + by 7.15 p.m. it was fairly quiet

1247 W 3290 200,000 (E) 8/14 J.B.C. &A. Forms/C. 2118/11.

Army Form C. 2118.

WAR DIARY
or
INTELLIGENCE SUMMARY

(Erase heading not required.)

Hour, Date, Place	Summary of Events and Information	Remarks and references to Appendices
5.7.15	During the day nothing of importance occurred. It was however reported that the German artillery used by the enemy at dawn at YPRES obliged the forcing of the 3rd Div. holding the eastern exit of the salient onwards and to withdraw. Nothing further heard to establish on the development of YPRES. Mainly cutting wires. No casualties. Fair weather. The situation in and near the salient to YPRES being unfavourable for the relief of troops the withdrawal to [unclear] in 3rd Div. Sig. Section ordered of No. 1.4. 2.3. 15th Chinese men & were to relieve in this [unclear] the order were issued and reporting the situation in and near the salient. Feb 5th 1945 to the [unclear] of the 20th Division. To [unclear] other Details who have been in reserve	

Army Form C. 2118.

WAR DIARY
or
INTELLIGENCE SUMMARY

(Erase heading not required.)

Instructions regarding War Diaries and Intelligence Summaries are contained in F.S. Regs., Part II. and the Staff Manual respectively. Title pages will be prepared in manuscript.

Hour, Date, Place	Summary of Events and Information	Remarks and references to Appendices
5-5-15	At 2 A.M. 2nd PPCLI's party were relieved by the MONMOUTH SHIRE Regt – The party had been pretty badly gassed but did not suffer to the same extent as W.R.R. or PPCLI. During the day the trenches & gun armament in G.H.Q. line [?] enemy against which to [?] only shell some damage. At 7.50 P.M. Hon. H. Maxton started off to relieve the 3rd Batts in support at the eastern end of BELLEWAARDE LAKE. The 3rd Batt: we had been relieved W.R.B. from the right section & the trenches R & L7 remaining on the left section. During the night a [?] challenge opened fire & [?] the [?] into [?] artillery [?] & [?] were fired and [?] shell (H.E.)	
6-5-15	A quiet day in the immediate neighbourhood. Our guns seemed on the whole to be rather more active. Nothing further to report.	
7-5-15	From about midnight 6-7" a hostile heavy battery from direction due south started shelling over a wide area with [?]	

Army Form C. 2118.

WAR DIARY
or
INTELLIGENCE SUMMARY

(Erase heading not required.)

Instructions regarding War Diaries and Intelligence Summaries are contained in F.S. Regs., Part II. and the Staff Manual respectively. Title pages will be prepared in manuscript.

Hour, Date, Place	Summary of Events and Information	Remarks and references to Appendices
8-5-15.	The day opens: on N. of BELLEWAARDE LAKE – Three shells continued promiscuous fire.	
2.40 A.M.	Heavy M.G. & Rifle fire from the direction of HILL 60 this was followed immediately by heavy gun fire in our sector into from field batteries due east. This fired down about dawn. (3.G.am) The day was fairly quiet in the immediate neighbourhood. At dusk the Battalion relieved the 3rd Batt^n in the trenches east of BELLEWAARDE LAKE & WOODS	
5.0.A.M	Heavy Howitzers opened on the front trenches – these continued steadily until 7 A.M. when a furious combined bombardment of field guns and howrs commenced. This heavy fire was maintained until almost 8.0 A.M. when traces were distinct.	
8.5 A.M	The bombardment slackened considerably. The French had been cut out & Communication by wire to the French had almost immediately afterwards the brigade line	

WAR DIARY or INTELLIGENCE SUMMARY

Army Form C. 2118.

(Erase heading not required.)

Instructions regarding War Diaries and Intelligence Summaries are contained in F.S. Regs, Part II. and the Staff Manual respectively. Title pages will be prepared in manuscript.

Hour, Date, Place	Summary of Events and Information	Remarks and references to Appendices
20	also went. The line to RB in support held until about 7.45 am	
8 am	The bombardment increased - especially about the centre of BELLEWAARDE WOOD where Patrol of C Coy went in support. Batt Headquarters were detached.	
8.30 am	Heavy rifle fire opened on the front & left - the front line which had suffered very heavily during the bombardment was now reinforced. Lt POOLE, ANTROBUS & HODGKINSON taking up companies. The remainder of C Coy - The whole Battalion was now in the firing line - One party took up a supply of ammunition	
8.40 am	Lt POOLE returned with information that infantry attack did not appear to be in our front	
8-45 am	German Artillery continued making BELLEWAARDE WOOD a perfect inferno, shelling with every sort of shell. Three orderlies from R.B. arrived to ask for help required. These returned with request for one company.	
8.50 am		
9.0 am	A lull in the artillery bombardment the little	

Army Form C. 2118.
(64)

WAR DIARY
or
INTELLIGENCE SUMMARY
(Erase heading not required.)

Instructions regarding War Diaries and Intelligence Summaries are contained in F. S. Regs., Part II. and the Staff Manual respectively. Title pages will be prepared in manuscript.

Hour, Date, Place	Summary of Events and Information	Remarks and references to Appendices
9.17 a.m.	Rifle fire was [?] but was heavier further north. A message received stated that enemy appeared to be massing in front of right of 2.D.H. firing (?) cooperate. Do it B.O.R.	
9.45 a.m.	Capt Bullen came in reported that the Scots Rif Hill 50 had been shelled while the men [?] it. Were annihilated & that the Germans had worked into it. Whilst explaining the situation Captain DALBY was wounded. This hill was a weak spot in the line taken the junction of trenches - PRELL.	
10.15 a.m.	A company of the 4 R.B. arrived & moved up to the junction Bus 16. fill up the gaps.	
10.20 a.m.	The situation so far as known 4 + B Coy in trench line. Rifles reserve supposedly D Coy regiment scattered but a few still left in left of front line. Enemy after Hill 50 held by enemy.	

1247 W 3290 200,000 (E) 8/14 J.B.C. & A. Forms/C. 2118/11.

Army Form C. 2118.

(65)

WAR DIARY
or
INTELLIGENCE SUMMARY
(Erase heading not required.)

Instructions regarding War Diaries and Intelligence Summaries are contained in F.S. Regs., Part II. and the Staff Manual respectively. Title pages will be prepared in manuscript.

Hour, Date, Place	Summary of Events and Information	Remarks and references to Appendices
	A & B Coys had also been strongly shelled (punished)	
11.0 a.m.	One Company of the R.B. was moving up to reinforce front line and another Company was in support in	
	"Crosby" Lane just west of BELLEWAARDE WOOD	
12.15 P.M.	All seemed quiet again.	
1.30 P.M.	Communication with the Brigade was re-established	
2.45 P.M.	Shelling recommenced but not with its former vehemence	
	Slackened again and continued until 5.0 p.m	
	About dusk several small patrols were sent out	
	from different points (?) of Trench & (?) Valence to the firing line	
	So far no could be ascertained the Battalion (A) suffered about	
	three hundred casualties (eighty with three officers killed & three	
	wounded.	
9-6-15	At 2.0 a.m information was received of a readjustment	
	of our line	

Army Form C. 2118.

66

WAR DIARY
or
INTELLIGENCE SUMMARY

(Erase heading not required.)

Instructions regarding War Diaries and Intelligence Summaries are contained in F. S. Regs., Part II. and the Staff Manual respectively. Title pages will be prepared in manuscript.

Hour, Date, Place	Summary of Events and Information	Remarks and references to Appendices
9.0 A.M	The battalion fell following back of the regiment on our left until its right rested on the N.W. corner of BELVEDERE LAKE. The left of the battalion was thus in the air & open to enfilade fire from HILL 50 & further WEST. The Battalion headquarters were thus in full view of this enemy on the NORTH & was such that it would be impossible to miss. Headquarters were therefore removed to the West of the dike where about 30 men had been rallied 300x & 4 R3 also had headquarters here. Bombardment (shells) not very heavy so infantry attack — This slackened towards 10 AM. The majority of it came & have been directed at FORGE (our) Ord(inances) towers &c. The bombardment was followed by a very weak infantry advance which was easily repulsed	

Army Form C. 2118.

(67)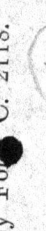

WAR DIARY
or
INTELLIGENCE SUMMARY

(Erase heading not required.)

Instructions regarding War Diaries and Intelligence Summaries are contained in F.S. Regs., Part II. and the Staff Manual respectively. Title pages will be prepared in manuscript.

Hour, Date, Place	Summary of Events and Information	Remarks and references to Appendices
	On the front of the Battalion normally infantry advance was against hun left from the direction of HILL 50. No troops were easily sighted at dawn & nearest escort – no further movement of the enemy being visible. Shortly after dawn four Germans suddenly appeared in our left trench as far a moment surprised the occupants who thought that they were prisoners men. On the interrogation scruple two of them managed to escape. They proved to be men of the 246th Res Inf Regt. Battalion Headquarters was now moved to HEDGE CHATEAU. Officers are being drawn to the Battalion & men available for the transmission of information. On all the shoot rifles was occupied in repairing trenches & making up rifles & ammunition.	[signature]

1247 W 3299 200,000 (E) 8/14 J.B.C. & A. Forms/C. 2118/11.

Army Form C. 2118.

WAR DIARY
or
INTELLIGENCE SUMMARY

(Erase heading not required.)

Hour, Date, Place	Summary of Events and Information	Remarks and references to Appendices
10 - 5 - 15.		
9.0. a.m.	At 5 a.m the enemy started shelling with heavy howitzers. Towards 7.0 am the bombardment increased in intensity. A very hot burst of Rifle & machine gun fire approaches. Observed to a few men of A Coy wounded etc falling back in support trench. These men were immediately reorganised in the support trench together with some R.B. reserves & reoccupied the front line. Lt. POOLE left headquarters & went up to the support.	
10.0 a.m.	Trench in front of the log hut in BEECHWARDS WOOD + took Lt. AMBROSUS and about 20 men up into the front line. The strength of battalion now appeared to be about 200 men.	
10.30 am	A very heavy battery opened from the direction of ST ELOI (and) MLR 60 - Another from the N.E. — field guns from E + N.E. A terrific bombardment was kept up until about 1.30 pm when 15 four-seven fell back on the country lane now held	

WAR DIARY or INTELLIGENCE SUMMARY

(Erase heading not required.)

Army Form C. 2118.

Hour, Date, Place | **Summary of Events and Information** | **Remarks and references to Appendices**

by R.B. CAMERONS + a company of 3rd M R R C
The BELLEWAARDE WOOD was now our almost impenetrable
obstacle - it was immediately decided to consolidate. The
enemy line + hold it with every available man.
Tho' this was bombarded the fire was not so accurate as
had been in the front line probably owing to difficulties of
communication + observation

The Camerons on our right by previous arrangement (obtained)
then left flank backwards to conform to our new line.
O.C. Camerons immediately pulled up two companies of
A + S Highs to man the line at HOOGE + two more
cops were sent up by R.O. TRDE in rear of HOOGE CHATEAU.
The situation after midday became so serious that the D.O.
Inf Bdes were appealed to for strong supports.
Two [?] in 1st & 2nd A&S Highs being sent up to STRODGE
arriving between 3 + 4 p.m.
The enemy again made no determined attack but merely

WAR DIARY
or
INTELLIGENCE SUMMARY
(Erase heading not required.)

Army Form C. 2118.

(70)

Hour, Date, Place	Summary of Events and Information	Remarks and references to Appendices
2.0 P.M.	forward in small parties & halting or falling back if met with infantry fire. A few of the enemy crept forward towards cavalry trench but no attack was made. From this moment things became quieter & the fight seemed to fizzle out. 3 Vi Bn RB from W bank of LAKE obtained good oblique fire on small parties under the woods & checked any further advance. This seemed to mark the limit of the enemy's aspirations for the day, as no further serious movements took place. A draft of 150 men under 2Lt HYLTON came up at about 9.30 P.M. & was taken into the G.H.Q. Line S of MENIN ROAD to be organised. Meanwhile orders had been received to withdraw the remnants of the battalion from the trenches & to return to the WEST of YPRES to reorganise.	

WAR DIARY or INTELLIGENCE SUMMARY

Army Form C. 2118.

Hour, Date, Place	Summary of Events and Information	Remarks and references to Appendices
	By midnight the battalion was drawn out to its number of about 100 which included stragglers & stretcher bearers. The C.O. (Major Majendie)s. Adjutant and 2 Lt ANTROBUS being the sole surviving officers. One machine gun very much knocked about was also brought away It's other being destroyed. Only three men of M.G. section remained. During the fighting of the period few deeds individual acts of gallantry were very numerous as is to be expected but evidence of the majority is not now available. As a unit the work of the battalion both officers & men was admirable & many messages (attached) of congratulation have been received from the higher commanders. The losses in the period this diary in R.W. & Missing amount'd to about 15 Officers + 478 R.F.	

WAR DIARY
or
INTELLIGENCE SUMMARY

(Erase heading not required.)

Army Form C. 2118.

Hour, Date, Place	Summary of Events and Information	Remarks and references to Appendices
11-5-15	Shortly after daylight the battalion learned at a bivouac west of YPRES but was later given orders to return to the transport at BUSSEBOOM which place was reached at about 1 P.M. Here the battalion lay down for the first genuine rest since	
12-5-15		
13-5-15	Battn. went to baths at REIGHINGHURST	
14-5-15	1.30 A.M. Received orders to move to a position near VLAMERTINGHE & there joining up with 7 P. C.L.I. form a complete battalion. 5.0 A.M. Raining hard - marched off arriving at HQ Reserve 1PM at 7.10 A.M. — No corn available to sleep any.	

Army Form C. 2113.

WAR DIARY
or
INTELLIGENCE SUMMARY
(Erase heading not required.)

Hour, Date, Place	Summary of Events and Information	Remarks and references to Appendices
7 P.M.	Very crowded places in barns sheds etc. P.REILLY arrived about 200 strong under LT H W NIVEN — MAJ MAZENDIE took command of the combined Battalion. The Battalion went off to relieve 4th T.R.B — passing guides at canal crossing MENIN road the relief being completed without casualties by 11.45 P.M.	[signature]
19.5.15	Very quiet until about 10 am when a little heavy shelling appeared to be directed on the trenches to L & R It then increased in intensity & went 10.45 a.m. but subsided & now appeared to be NE heavy battery (enemy) in action. Shells of our own guns (probably 9.2 - and 6 inch) passing over & bursting in direction of STIRLING CASTLE at intervals.	

Army Form C. 2118.

(72)

WAR DIARY
or
INTELLIGENCE SUMMARY

(Erase heading not required.)

Instructions regarding War Diaries and Intelligence Summaries are contained in F. S. Regs., Part II. and the Staff Manual respectively. Title pages will be prepared in manuscript.

Hour, Date, Place	Summary of Events and Information	Remarks and references to Appendices
16-6-15	High velocity gun (Bing-Bang) fired at intervals through out the afternoon — otherwise all quiet 12-10 of yesterday	
	About 3.0 a.m. a few shells were dropped about and at 7.30 a.m. a trench battery of our own started dropping a few dangerously short — (short-shots) again very close firing evidently a little business between the opposing artillerise from 5 to 8 P.M. — Enemy suspicious rather less active they Observed quiet.	
	About 9 P.M. the no. 18th CAV BDE relieved by no. 9th Kentish with a view to taking over on 17th	
	9.10 P.M. a burst of rapid fire opened to some action on the front of the Canadians to our right	

1247 W 3209 200,000 (b) 8/14 J.B.C.&A. Forms/C. 2118/11.

Army Form C. 2118.

WAR DIARY
or
INTELLIGENCE SUMMARY

(Erase heading not required.)

Instructions regarding War Diaries and Intelligence Summaries are contained in F. S. Regs., Part II. and the Staff Manual respectively. Title pages will be prepared in manuscript.

Hour, Date, Place	Summary of Events and Information	Remarks and references to Appendices
17 – 5 – 17	Q. Very quiet day - A little gunning at 3 P.M. and again at 6.45 P.M. - Our batteries dropping a few heavy shells - Relief by ourselves completed by 11.45 P.M. Battalion set out by companies for BUSSEBOOM	
18 – 5 – 17	Arrived BUSSEBOOM - weather rather unpleasant but worth the trouble of a longer rest nobody minded much. Major B willing to reguale us with beer. Butter supplied by 15th British French	
19 – 5 – 17	Reorganization.	
20 – 5 – 17		
21 – 5 – 17	A trek up somewhere by Gand Mascon Verley	
22 – 5 – 17	a ploy to the Brigade	
23 – 5 – 17	new gullies billes & 2/Lt F Bevan joined the Battalion	

Army Form C. 2118.

76

WAR DIARY
or
INTELLIGENCE SUMMARY
(Erase heading not required.)

Instructions regarding War Diaries and Intelligence Summaries are contained in F.S. Regs., Part II. and the Staff Manual respectively. Title pages will be prepared in manuscript.

Hour, Date, Place	Summary of Events and Information	Remarks and references to Appendices
24th May	3.30 AM Order received to be in readiness to move at half an hour's notice. 5 AM orders to march to Brigade to Poperinghe Ypres road to be in readiness to support 28th Division who had detrained this morning. Battalion waited all day on the road W & E of VLAMERTINGE and about 5 PM received orders to form the support to a Brigade counter attack against the still line of trenches from SW corner of BELLEWARDE LAKE — MENIN ROAD. The 3rd KRR to attack on the left, the 4/KRR on the right supported respectively by 1/S4. and 4/KRR. The Brigade moved via INDISSTRAAT and railway line S of YPRES to GHQ line E of YPRES. Great delay was experienced by the approach getting a purview to HQ and this position was not reached till 10 PM. Orders were then thought unnecessary to the attack. On returning we halted during hours of remaining troops let we sustained no casualties beyond.	

WAR DIARY or INTELLIGENCE SUMMARY

Army Form C. 2118.

77

Hour, Date, Place	Summary of Events and Information	Remarks and references to Appendices
24th (continued)	The push when met the 3rd KRRC & 4th RB should attack as previously ordered but that the KSLI and another should support in counter attack by the 84th Bde on BELLEWARDE FARM and RAILWAY WOOD. The Bn advanced after considerable delay and about 1.30 AM in four lines but never got touch with the 84th Bde except small parties who were found behind hedges. The KSLI were in our left front. On reaching a small stream 200x W of WITTE POORT FARM in Enfilade Machine gun & musketry fire broke our assembly to indicate that the enemy was being delivered by 84th Bde. The Battalion then deployed into 4 lines & continued to advance. The firing line which twice greater Bellewre crossed the road E of	

WAR DIARY or INTELLIGENCE SUMMARY

Army Form C. 2118.

78

Hour, Date, Place	Summary of Events and Information	Remarks and references to Appendices

25th WITTEPORT FARM. Enemy were unable to advance further than 50 yards owing to machine gun & rifle fire. A party of about 50 men made an attempt to advance up the hillside but failed and charged to within 25 yards of German trench. This party on perceiving our numbers & 1st Battalion fell back with severe casualties & 1st Battalion in turn of WITTEPORT FARM. Counter party of NF were to form up Grid - Billeau in hope of being launched to about 12 noon & got about 20 yds from German trench when they had an eye on men (about 1 per head) on to keep down flank was. The OC RSLI then ordered troops forward to not hold company up to second line to leave one Coy to help and take to up to farm in cooperation to RSLI and to hold to same line.

Col Beddington

WAR DIARY
or
INTELLIGENCE SUMMARY

(Erase heading not required.)

Army Form C. 2118.

Hour, Date, Place	Summary of Events and Information	Remarks and references to Appendices
25th (cont)	of Bn taken back to GHQ line S of MENIN ROAD in be considered the general position. Nothing to be further attempted all day on probability. In four to live comrade was obtained chiefly by daylight. The recoveries on received at assembly at time Frulé-Bellis Hilaire + 2/Lt Mackay proceeded to bring his men to rest in a different compound to held the line. They remained in this position all night they were relieved + returning to GHQ line. 2/Lt Baker on killed & the deriver of the latrine wounded at casualties amounted to roughly 150. Our Bn was ordered to dig a new line at right [angles] from N corner of ZOUAVE WOOD NW [towards] MENIN road in conjunction with 3/KRR + 4/RR. 150 men under 2/Lt Pereira dug this line	

WAR DIARY or INTELLIGENCE SUMMARY

Army Form C. 2118. 80

(Erase heading not required.)

Hour, Date, Place	Summary of Events and Information	Remarks and references to Appendices
26.5.15	250 yards in length & inspected it. The Bn. then were relieved at 10 PM by 1st 9th Gurkha Rifles & marched back to BASSEBOOM the relief being carried out successfully & arrived there about 3 AM [on 27th and but in houses having the men who had lost their arms front of the way.	
27.5.15	Reorganization. Capt. Emley went on 1m sick leave.	
28 –	Rest'd at BASSEBOOM	
29 –		
30 –		
31 – 6 – 15	The Division having, under the new organization, come under the command of the III Corps — the 80th Bde. marched this day to LOCRE en route for ARMENTIÈRES	

CASUALTY LIST.

Casualties 4.5.15.

Killed. R888 A/c H Thornley. R10047 Rfn H Cooke.
Wounded. Y1858 Rfn T Davis. 8273 Rfn J Bradshaw. Y1461 Rfn W Scratton. 10931 L/c C Landgridge. A657 L/s G Woods. 4461 Rfn E Wilkinson. 1436 Rfn J Gill. 4801 Rfn S Brown. R 6333 Rfn H Bishop. Y381 Rfn M Collins. A 32 Rfn A Church. 5419 Rfn J O'Sullivan. R5637 Rfn E Lester. 3189 Rfn E Priest.

Casualties 5.5.15.

Killed. 7188 Rfn S Bennett. A1224 Rfn H Stevens.
Wounded. 9366 Rfn J Cassiddy. 2878 Rfn G Morris. R10178 Rfn J Turner. 9827 Rfn H Bullock. 2463 Rfn J Wilkins. R8774 Rfn M Williams. A260 Rfn W Bryant. R5344 J Marney. 7070 Rfn H Nelson. A134 Cpl J Stokes. Y707 Rfn J Green. 6702 Rfn E Warren. 8773 Rfn H Cook.

Casualties 6.5.15.

Killed. 8993 Rfn H Moss. 9907 Rfn Eyre.
Wounded. Y1837 L/c G Hawkes. 9997 Rfn W Davis. Y1044 Rfn W Blundell. 9341 Rfn J Moore.

Killed 7.5.15.

9613 Rfn J Cooper.

Casualties 8 to 10.5.15.

Killed.
Lieut. L.H.ST A King. Lieut. D.F.F. Shennan. 2Lieut. N.M.K. Bertie. 2Lieut. H. C.M. Farmer.
10162 Rfn A Parman. 10484 Rfn T Cain. 11403 Rfn A Stevenson. Y211 Rfn B Ling R8987 A/c W Reid. 6702 Rfn E Warren. 4309 C.S.M.J. Berridge. 6789 A/s O Valerio. 9667 L/c B Williamson. 10791 Rfn J Bloodworth. 1346 Rfn J Burton. 8233 Rfn P Carroll. 9613 Rfn J Cooper. 9238 L/c R Ettery. 9767 Rfn J Hoole. 9156 Rfn C Lewis. 9490 L/c C Nicholls. 5646 Rfn R Johnson. 3576 Rfn J Roberts R7476 Rfn A Johnson. 9654 Rfn J Robson. Y1486 Rfn F Newmna. 9976 Sgt A Shute. 7845 L/s G Horne. 8434 Bgr L Burnham. 914 Rfn W Boswell. R10201 Rfn F Cairns. Y585 Rfn F Checkley. 4552 Rfn J Danton. R10203 Rfn W Hill. 8489 Rfn H Lewis. 11661 Rfn W Miles. Y803 Rfn W Osment. 10454 Rfn G Porter. R10172 Rfn R Taylor. 8425 Rfn C Ward. R10191 Rfn A Wilson. R10176 Rfn G Wilson. 9060 Cpl T Long. 2799 A/c T Clarke. 8567 Rfn R Nolan. 10097 Rfn F Smith. 10443 Rfn A Tuck. Y791 Rfn S Wadham. 9091 Rfn J Walker. 1205 C.S.M.G. Bentley. 635 L/c T Edwards 5661 L/c G Grizzell. 11568 Rfn J Cooper. 11582 Rfn J Tickridge. 10477 Rfn J Hutchins. 11737 Rfn W Long. 7102 Rfn C Weston. 6813 T Graham. Y1186 Rfn S Broughton. 7808 Rfn J Hill. A410 Rfn W Lewis. 11968 Rfn J Goose. 8169 Rfn J Mead. 8141 Rfn J Roberts. R7078 Rfn E Williams. 7200 Bdm J Matthews. 11593 Rfn C Eggleton. 11327 Rfn A Cheeseman. Y168 Rfn T Ainsworth.

Wounded. Captain H.W.M. Watson. Captain G.T. Dalby. 2nd Lieut. C.G. Haynes. 2nd Lieut. R.J. Hodgkinson. 2nd Lieut. C. Smith. Lieut. A.E. Lawrence. Lieut. J. Knight.
8185 L/s J. Britton. 6026 L/c F. Robinson. Y816 Rfn W. Wilton. Y755 Rfn H Hetherington. 8432 Cpl E. Hennessy. 3274 L/c S. Hare. 6948 Rfn J. Bartlett. 7672 Bdm H. Smith. 9640 C.Q.M.S. H. Shone. 10401 Rfn G Colman. 2825 Rfn F. Floyd. 10067 Rfn J Hines. 10014 Rfn T. Lindsell. 9990 Rfn G. Rogers. Y1741 Rfn G. Wright. 2754 Sgt C. Williams. 11591 Rfn J. Martin. Y485 Rfn R. Davis. 8861 Rfn J. Flint. 3675 Rfn J. Evans. 9710 Rfn J. Edge. 2884 Rfn J. Ford. 9078 Rfn E. Bassham. 9301 Bdm J. Fitzgerald. Y817 Rfn G. Collingwood. 10079 Rfn T. Durant.. 10045 Rfn C. Davey. 9228 L/c C. Gilligan. Y992 Rfn R. Nelson. 7987 Sgt B. Cloake. Y787 Rfn J. Perry. 7878 Rfn H. Wilkinson. 9285 Rfn C. Stratton. 10294 Rfn M. Hogan. 9221 Rfn H. Payne. 2558 Rfn J. Keough. 7588 Bdm C. Southgate 10116 L/c J. Eves. 7988 Rfn G. Brereton. 160 Rfn G. Keats. 7738 Rfn A. Edmonds.

```
-------------------------------------------------------------------------
   Regl.No.    Rank and Name.              Nature of Casualty.
-------------------------------------------------------------------------
```

Wounded.   Casualties 8 to 10.5.15 continued.

4610 Rfn A.Healey. 1331 Rfn J.Hughes. R6237 Rfn R.Phybus. 8486 L/c J.Walker.
11702 Cpl A.Austin.8684 Sgt E.Leach.8890 A/s A.Hester.4829 Cpl C.Mason.9109
A/c J.Woodall.8648 L/c W.Robinson.Y1679 Rfn C.Attwood.R10192 Rfn G.Beddoes.
9567 Rfn H.Bowen.7924 Rfn J.Brewer. 9066 Rfn A.Burniston.7777 Rfn H.
Bartholomew. 9989 Rfn E.Clarke. Y1485 Rfn N.Cooper. 7497 Rfn A.Creamer.
Y660 Rfn W.Crump. Y1621 Rfn T.Clements. 7939 Rfn W.Crittenden.9135 Rfn P.
Daley.R10184 Rfn J.Day.R10187 L/c A.Dendy.R10296 Rfn L.Farnworth.Y1215 Rfn G.
Fern. 8701 Rfn T.Gelder.10187 Rfn W.Gilbert.9236 Rfn E.Goodall.R9928 Rfn P.
Haley.10070 Rfn E.Hoadley.8552 Rfn R.Hampson. R10193 Rfn G.Harness.8992
Rfn G.Healey.Y365 Rfn A.Larkin.7854 Rfn S.Lindley.R10173 Rfn C.Livingstone
R10181 Rfn P.Paul.R10188 Rfn G.Pinkerton.4164 Rfn A.Roberts.R10198 Rfn Ross.
R10197 L/c J.Mackay.4347 Rfn G.Morris. 9876 Rfn F.Palmer. R10194 Rfn R.Parnell
7529 Rfn E.Rowell. 647 Bdm A.Smith.R10295 Rfn A.Speers. 7937 Rfn H.Tarver.
8007 Rfn G.Watkins. R10182 Rfn E.Whittenbury. 3348 Rfn T.Powell.R10202 L/c W.
Niven. 862 C.S.M.W.Bulman. 1134 Sgt T.Ismay. 8506 Sgt C.Noble. 8208 Sgt J.
Pugsley. A657 L/s G.Woods. 7921 Cpl A.Ladson. 1506 L/c A.Baxter. 10139 L/c
H.Johnson. 7032 L/c W.Wilding.7800 A/c A.Woodhead. 6414 Bdm F.Buckland.
A1437 Rfn G.Acton. 9760 Rfn A.Banks. 10199 Rfn A.Barneveld. 10282 Rfn F.Bligh.
9417 Rfn J.Boorer. 11596 Rfn S.Bristowe. 10473 Rfn J.Burgess. 10259 Rfn S.
Camp. Y312 Rfn J.Charnock. Y810 A/c A.Clarke.7893 Rfn E.Davies. Y1834 Rfn A.
Davies. R7967 Rfn S.Dean. 12055 Rfn G.Gibbs. 7908 Rfn P.Gilby.Y427 Rfn A.
Graham. 9292 Rfn H.Hadley. 11809 Rfn T.Hanson. Y1731 Rfn J.Harrison. Y1209
Rfn G.Hateley. Y189 Rfn G.Holmes. 10213 L/c P.Jones. R5821 Rfn J.Jukes.
12097 Rfn W.Lane. Y1246 Rfn W.Lawley. 8408 Rfn C.Lewis. Y157 Rfn A".Lord.
8140 Rfn J.Maden. 8737 Rfn D.Margeson. Y270 Rfn C.McGowan.8035 Rfn H.Milling-
Ham. 8675 Rfn J.O'Connell. Y186 Rfn G.Ogden. R7269 Rfn E.Overall. R10810
Rfn A.Pacey. 6000 Rfn W.Page. 8307 Rfn S.Pittock. A3189 Rfn E.Priest.7282
Rfn R.Phipps. Y119 Rfn F.Pink. W1474 Rfn S.Pridie. 11460 Rfn S.Pumphrey.
7267 Rfn F.Rogers. 10662 Rfn J.Shewry. 9187 Rfn J.Slater. 566 Rfn H.Smith.
R10963 Rfn W.Sorrell. R10178 Rfn J.Turner. Y1020 Rfn W.Veasey. 8738 Rfn
E.Waddington. 7058 Rfn J.Warren. 6724 Rfn Weatherill. 12010 Rfn A.White.
7730 Rfn O.Whiteside. 10381 Rfn E.Willows. 7851 L/c J.Wilson. 10061 Rfn A.
Wright. 10556 Rfn A.Young. 1677 Rfn W.Cannon. 8612 Sgt S.Allsopp.8410 Cpl
R.Wilson.11613 Rfn G.Drew. Y309 Rfn W.Leyland.11742 Rfn J.Pettifer.Y1495
Rfn R.Matthews.8804 Rfn E.Jones. 8438 Rfn RMTownsend. 6300 Bgr J.Brown.
11034 Rfn E.Calnan.Y326 Rfn G.Foyle. 495 Rfn F.Kent. 10284 Rfn H.Payne.A3311
J.Delicate.Y1188 Rfn H.Smith.1132 Rfn J.Walker.8642 T.Cleall.114 L/c T.
Pearce. 8798 Rfn C.Wigley. 10496 Rfn A.Clarke. 7383 Rfn H.Davis. 3374 Rfn
E.Dodd.1736 Rfn H.Young. Y1848 Rfn F.Gilson.12058 Rfn W.Hancock.7792 Rfn G
Clever. Y1409 Rfn C.Tatnell.Y728 Rfn H.Walker. 7796 Rfn A.Richardson.
10193 Rfn W.Moore. 8228 A/c T.Hartley. Y1103 Rfn J.Smith. R7013 Rfn C.Mc
Allister. 10587 Rfn W.Peacock. 7942 Rfn J.Begley.Y337 Rfn Cox.8513 Rfn W.
W.Croucher. 12103 Rfn S.Cooper. 8459 Rfn W.Ashington.8452 Rfn M.Grady.7763
Rfn T.Tucker. 1285 Cpl W.Stephenson.8473 A/c T.Medhurst.6073 Rfn Brackstone.
9302 Rfn R.Thompson. R10843 Rfn Young. 9344 L/c R.Dobson.R7463 Rfn E.Lilley.
11664 L/c Williams.11519 Rfn T.Brindley. 10501 Rfn W.Smith. 9040 Rfn L.Harris
953 Rfn A.Bridges. 10533 Rfn J.Midlam. 8375 Rfn J.Redmond. 9198 Rfn E.Marr.
4835 Rfn H.Hilton. 9332 Rfn A.Penn. 9002 Rfn J.Harford. 8469 Rfn A.Newton.
8551 Rfn C.Harrison. Y137 Rfn J.Duckworth.

Wounded and Missing.   2Lieut.D.Morton.
2193 Sgt T.Thundercliffe. R9929 Rfn J.Barry. 11281 Rfn A.Barford. R10180 Rfn
N.Loder. 9781 Rfn J McKeown.

Missing. 2Lieuts.J.S.Poole,M.B.Hope,G.T.Croft-Smith.
10398 A/c C.Bailey. 11580 Rfn L.Barnard. 10727 Rfn R.Boyce. Y218 Rfn T.Brown.
A3241 Rfn G.Baverstoke.11920 Rfn A.Best. R10841 Rfn A.Howard. 5937 Rfn J.
Handley. 475 Rfn A.Jones. 9673 Rfn A.Jones. 6880 A/s J.Kaye. Y690 L/c G.
Monument. 10096 Rfn C.Menzies. Y774 Rfn A.Nicholls.7920 Rfn W.Plant. Y1109
Rfn T.Clarke. 7845 L/c H.Fuller. 10481 Rfn A.Farnham. Y999 Rfn W.Hudson.
R10186 Cpl E Rogers. 9982 Rfn A.Antley. 7708 Rfn A Brooks. 8724 Rfn J.Boyles.
12066 Rfn J.Brown. R5630 Rfn H.Bolton.A823 Rfn W.Ballard. 9897 Rfn B.Coleman.

```
Regl.No.    Rank and Name.                    Nature of casualty.
```

Missing continued.

11589 Rfn P Harding, 8673 Bgr A Jones, 9712 Rfn G Jones, 877 Rfn W James, R5982 Rfn J Keyser, R10860 Rfn C Marsh, R10831 Rfn E Nicholson, 11950 Rfn E Cope, 8687 Rfn P Carroll, Y788 Rfn G Cooper, 5011 Rfn M Donovan, 5728 Rfn A Frow, 1681 Rfn A Hibbert, 799 Rfn P Haley, 9573 Rfn F Rose, Y1768 Rfn W Styles, 9950 L/c F Tricker, 6038 Rfn A Ulph, Y974 Rfn C Wilson, R10169 Sgt G Bailey, 10254 L/c J Arnold, 9012 L/c G Stokes, 3284 Rfn A Carter, 7685 Rfn J Connor, 4224 Rfn C Foley, 11423 Rfn W Fry, 5845 Rfn J Grimson, 8252 Rfn T Gibson, Y1067 Rfn T Gratton, 11015 Rfn S Halsey, Y717 Rfn J Howarth, Y1258 Rfn J Jones, R8730 Rfn F Kiddy, 11646 Rfn T Lewis, R10171 Rfn N Millard, 10108 Rfn N Parslow, 4453 Rfn N Robinson, R6379 Rfn G South, Y1161 Rfn P Southgate, 11163 Rfn W Storr, R10261 Rfn G Turner, 8928 Rfn P Ward, 11468 Rfn W Shephard, 7466 Rfn W Turner, 4866 Rfn W West, Y997 Rfn J Williams, 8814 Rfn A Preston, 9211 Cpl J Fargher, 11429 L/c A Berridge, 10865 L/c G Surridge, 9437 Rfn A Bowler, R10196 Rfn S Cutbush, 8098 Rfn J Davis, 1005 L/c E Francis, 7896 Rfn A Fuller, A3541 Rfn G Gamble, 4810 Rfn T Gratton, Y1193 Rfn A Hall, Y403 Rfn B Holder, 9684 Rfn T Jeavons, A1353 Rfn D Jobe, R6327 Rfn J King, R8748 Rfn C Longworth, 6845 Rfn F Marriott, 8492 Rfn L Pemberton, 268 Rfn N Slater, 11271 Rfn W Smith, 1270 Rfn S Stark, 7527 Rfn A Townsend, 11700 Rfn N Waite, Y802 Rfn N West, 887 Rfn Woolerson, 11011 Rfn E Cummings, 8647 Rfn B Binley, 11575 Rfn W Archer, 7963 Rfn W Battle, 9386 Rfn F Clarke, 5548 Rfn E Edmonds, 7914 Rfn E Gates, 3095 Rfn J Green, R3215 Rfn L Helliwell, Y1196 Rfn J Jennings, 9014 L/c W Kelly, 12036 Rfn C Mooney, Y363 Rfn W Myatt, 10173 Rfn W O'Connor, A1571 Rfn F Poppy, 9427 Rfn L Richardson, 4872 Rfn F Smith, R7959 Rfn J Starkey, A3388 Rfn E Spragg, Y1727 Rfn A Tipler, 2463 Rfn J Wilkins, Y1793 Rfn W Chambers, Y185 Rfn W Hayes, 8906 Rfn C Scott, A5022 Rfn M Rock, Y188 Rfn J Rogerson, Y418 Rfn F Hill, 10588 L/c A Rogers, Y1838 Rfn J Wood, R4530 Rfn A Baxter, Y1835 Rfn E Davies, Y495 Rfn E Garbutt, 8808 Rfn P Golder, Y631 Rfn B Haliday, 11838 Rfn W Hill, Y795 Rfn J Jones, 8192 Rfn J Miller, 10089 Rfn W Moss, Y1720 T O'Hara, Y726 Rfn J Perry, 5028 Rfn J Reed, 10825 Rfn G Saunders, Y190 Rfn E Smith, 7127 Rfn W Talbot, R10757 Rfn S Stacey, A63 Rfn A Taylor, 10135 L/c A York, 4816 Rfn A Evans, 11479 Rfn H King, Y1665 Rfn J Jago, Y1472 Rfn H Murray, 10486 Rfn A Clarke, Y1051 Rfn T Blank, 1359 Rfn S Bracewell, 10731 Rfn A James, 4012 Rfn S Brandon, 12153 Rfn T Dunn, 7625 Rfn J Ashby, Y1027 Rfn W Thorpe, 9944 Rfn G Martin, 9755 Rfn H Steeles, 485 Rfn F Hadley, 8415 Rfn H Hosker, Y1052 Rfn W Baven, 8152 Rfn J Wilkins, 12183 Rfn A Pearson, 3899 Rfn R Binks, 749 Rfn A Barrett, Y874 Rfn W Yeowell, 12165 Rfn C Green, 11199 Rfn W Goddard, 10781 Rfn J Byrne.
Died of wounds 11th A3093 Rfn A Phillips.

Casualties 15th 16th May 1915.

8039 Rfn A Hawthorne, killed 15th.
9119 Rfn J Gilraine, 6935 Bdm S Griffin, wounded 16th.
R9544 Rfn W Cliff, 9427 Rfn G Early, wounded 15th.

Casualties 25th May 1915.

Killed. 8456 L/c R Courts, 8662 L/c A Wareing, 8547 L/c E Rogers, 9806 Sgt T Scott, Y171 Rfn T Atherton, R7059 Rfn T Wells, 8534 Rfn A Ansell, 6274 Rfn E Goldring, 3029 Rfn S Chalnan, 12163 Rfn Howarth, 5040 Rfn G Simson.
WOUNDED. 8427 Sgt H Wilding, 946 Rfn P Ryan, 7070 Rfn H Nelson, 5378 Rfn H Norton, 10179 Rfn W Collins, 8548 Cpl G Pullen, 10656 Rfn E Upton, 10378 Rfn E Heath, Y2693 Rfn G Redfern, Y1706 Rfn A Watson, 10386 Rfn J Dunnings, 4761 Rfn E Hemley, R9521 L/s G Trevor, 2292 L/c H Douglas, R7893 Rfn E John, 10553 Rfn H Dann, 7030 L/c W Brooks, 241 Rfn W Miller, 320 Rfn A Atkins, 12168 Rfn A Butler, 8424 Sgt R Fernley, 10157 L/c H Johnson, 8175 Rfn J Menday, 5285 Rfn J Brown, R7419 Rfn E Scattergood, R7476 Rfn S Willey, 10365 Rfn B Findlater, Y1603 Rfn F Critch, 4425 Cpl B Ashley, 11779 Rfn Holmes, 10227 Rfn G Fowler, 6148 Sgt H Edmunds, 7717 Rfn F Johnson, 6255 L/c L Reed, 538 Rfn G Mackenzie, 4944 Rfn Buddin, 10093 Rfn G Wilds, 10401 Rfn G Colman, 9501 L/c E Marr, 11396 Rfn J Judd, 9836 Rfn F Ratcliffe, 12253 Rfn A Howarde, 4420 Cpl J Jacobs, 8900@868 8469 Bgr C Holder, 9888 A/c SM S Swann (wounded and missing) 9278 L/c R Dunn, 8047 Rfn H Addey, 10212 Rfn Theed, 8626 L/c James, Y798 Rfn T Moyce, 11778 Rfn M Middleton, 1181 Rfn W Mumford, Y1248 Rfn W Tomkin, R7408 Rfn P Hart, 9157 L/c G Childs, R9307 Rfn Tranter, 10727 Rfn Boyce, Y549 Rfn A Harley.
Wounded and Missing. Y4935 Rfn Smith.
Missing believed killed. R7157 Rfn D Samworth.

Regl.No.   Rank and Name.   Nature of Casualty.

Missing, 25th May 1915.

11544 L/c B Symes,8603 L/c F Duckworth,11221 L/c L Russ,7731 L/c A Arter,
12073 Rfn P Blaney,11791 Rfn W Grudgington,Y1708 Rfn F Dyson,R8740 Rfn S
Drewell,11423 Rfn W Fry,7218 Rfn E Morton,R8836 Rfn C Stanley,9295 Rfn G
Stringer,7340 Rfn W Buffield,R7154 Rfn J Haywood,943 Rfn J Waldron,9185
Rfn H Woods,6825 Rfn W Willis,R7414 Rfn A Park,1280 Rfn T Edmonds,5367
Rfn A Bloor,9804 Rfn J Clarkson,7988 Rfn J Marshall,10189 Rfn B Gardner,
R7359 Rfn R Plunkett,9345 Cpl T Chalmers,994 Rfn J Tidy,Y571 Rfn C McCann,
10445 Rfn C Drake,11821 Rfn W Ashwood,1042 Rfn V Groome,Y1887 Rfn A White,
12232 Rfn J Galcroft,R7061 Rfn T Webster,R7421 Rfn G Fowkes,7943 Rfn S
Bramley,Y119 Rfn F Pink,Y1754 Rfn T Lea,4890 Rfn E Taylor,9774 Rfn G Farrell,
70914 Rfn W Harper,11388 Rfn G Hill,8548 Rfn C Brothers,R7481 Rfn W Price,
R7714 Rfn J Shaw,A3000 Rfn H Newman,Y166 Rfn B Hemley,727 Rfn P Wilkinson,
8120 Rfn W Green,7750 Rfn E Jarrett,R10183 Rfn A Bursill,R5812 Rfn F Dodson,
R7973 Rfn A Doyle,Y1784 Rfn W Copestick,Y1807 Rfn J Worthington,8311 Rfn
J Clarke,6416 Rfn J Jones,A588 Rfn J Cantlin,10158 Rfn F James,8429 Rfn C
Smith,R1940 Rfn J Berrington,6638 Rfn J Barlow,R7942 Rfn W Walker,12174 Rfn
G Castle,8752 Rfn Thurlwell,R7284 Rfn J Baker,Y811 Rfn Fox,10502 Rfn King,
R9702 Rfn Thornton,9933 Rfn Cattell,9173 Rfn J Cook,Y1460 Rfn Clay,8463
Rfn W Nickson,6966 6934 L/c H Grubb,R8336 Rfn Williams,12247 Rfn W Fowler,
11288 Rfn Jefferies,R9932 Rfn Lowther,10792 Rfn W Baker,9928 Rfn W Kemp,
R9280 Rfn Walton,R9469 Rfn Westgate,5499 Rfn Neal,R7966 Rfn Meynell,R7953
Rfn Kent,10242 Rfn Hart,R4123 Rfn Doward.

Killed. 2Lieut.F.A.F.Baines.   Wounded. 2Lieut.F.Walton.

80th Infantry Brigade.

27th Division.

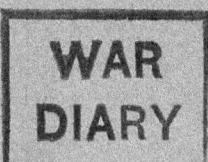

4th BATTN. THE KING'S ROYAL RIFLE CORPS.

J U N E

1 9 1 5

Attached:

Casualty List.

INTELLIGENCE SUMMARY

81.

Hour, Date, Place	Summary of Events and Information	Remarks and references to Appendices
1–6–15	(Continued) March to near STEENWERCK – during the afternoon officers & other representatives went in to see the trenches to be taken over.	
2–6–15	4.15 P.M. Marched for the ARMENTIERES regarding quarter asylum at 7.15 P.M. – Men had billets and had tea – The trenches were then taken over from the 2nd London Regt. the relief being complete by 11.25 P.M. The trenches were in a way better than any they were in yet seen. Now 12 to 15 say – they were strongly compatable & a bombardment by day or night – They were soft however in all parts made to resist a bombardment, being lots much of the nature of breast works.	
3–6–15	A very quiet day nothing to report	

1247 W 3299 200,000 (E) 8/14 J.B.C. & A.   Forms/C. 2118/11.

INTELLIGENCE SUMMARY

(Erase heading not required.)

Hour, Date, Place	Summary of Events and Information	Remarks and references to Appendices
4-6-15	A draft under Major Tryon 149 NCOs & Men arrived	
5-6-15	Quiet until 7.15 PM when a volley rang (battery opened) fire & fired about 30 or 40 rounds — no damage	
(6+7) 6-15	B.Sk absolutely quiet days — The draft worked on trenches & behind the line.	
8-6-15.	Draft again worked all day, & after dark the bat'n was relieved by 2 K.S.L.I., the relief being carried out by midnight. Total casualties for the tour — Lt PEREIRA Somerset LI (attached) slightly wounded 2 Rfm Killed 1 Rfm (Wounded) Battalion moved into billets in the Lunatic Asylum	

INTELLIGENCE SUMMARY

(Erase heading not required.)

Hour, Date, Place	Summary of Events and Information	Remarks and references to Appendices
ARMENTIERES 8th–11th June	Remained in billets until night of 11th when we went into the trenches in the EPINETTE Section. 1 Company 8th Battn Royal Fusiliers came in with us for instruction	
12–6–15	9.15–9.45 am a 6" howitzer sent about a dozen shells into EPINETTE. – Royal Fusilier Company relieved by another 1st Company Royal Fusilier Company relieved by another	
13–6–15	A very quiet day. – a small amount of shig-being but otherwise nothing to report. – 1st Company Royal Fusiliers went in by Platoons.	
14–6–15	Nothing special to report – at about 10.30 a.m. a heavy Howitzer fired 20 shells (probably 6") on the line south of the EPINETTE salient	
15–6–15	An extremely quiet day. An enemy working party was fired on during the night – nothing else to report	[signature]

INTELLIGENCE SUMMARY.

(Erase heading not required.)

(B4)

Hour, Date, Place	Summary of Events and Information	Remarks and references to Appendices
Near ARMENTIERES 16-6-15.	Nothing to report - A patrol went out during the normal hours to a napnea sap in front of EPINETTE but found it to be an old disused communication trench	
17-6-15.	Day again quiet. The enemy displayed flags in front of 74 and indulged in a certain amount of cheering but nothing more bellicose occurred. At night 1st Battalion was relieved by K.S.L.I. A Coy Capt BELLEW and two platoons of B were left in support. The remainder of the battalion went back to the Lunatic Asylum.	[signature]
10ᵏ 23-6-15	Remained in Rest Sunday, Oignies & Irriscourt reserve in period 2 Cpls 8th Batt Queens attached for instructions	

Hour, Date, Place	Summary of Events and Information	Remarks and references to Appendices
23-6-15	9. P.M. Left to take over EPINETTE section of the line held by 1st S.W.B. - Relief was completed by 12.25AM	
24-6-15	A few field gun shells were fired near battalion headquarters & the wound going — being seen in EPINETTE otherwise nothing to report.	
25-6-15	A quiet day nothing to report — Captain M.L.S. Clements arrived with a draft of 19 NCOs-RR	
26-6-15	About 10.30 am Enemy shelled the EPINETTE with fire Guns + Howitzers. Hostile aeroplane seen over the line but was turned by fire – a good deal of sniper presence was indulged in during the day – Except therein 16 to Army some work in front of our forward Apple the EPINETTE salient – machine gun trenches supplied sap. At about dusk – Enemy working parties were fired on being 16 night – Battalion relieved by 3 W.R.R.C. Complete by 1.30 AM 28-6-15.	

Army Form C. 2118.

86

WAR DIARY
or
INTELLIGENCE SUMMARY.

(Erase heading not required.)

Instructions regarding War Diaries and Intelligence Summaries are contained in F. S. Regs., Part II. and the Staff Manual respectively. Title pages will be prepared in manuscript.

Hour, Date, Place	Summary of Events and Information	Remarks and references to Appendices
Noven 27-6-15	C. Coy under Capt Tryon & one Platoon D Coy remained in support.	
28-6-15 to 1-7-15	The battalion remained in trenches in the Asylum — on night of 29th the above detachment was relieved by the remainder of D Coy & 2 Platoons of B. under Capt H.O. Curtis —	Addenda appended

CASUALTY LIST.

12164 Rfn G Wallace, Killed 2.6.1915
2nd Lieut. G.W.T.Pereria, Som, Light Infy, Wounded 6.6.15.
4944 Rfn W Sheppard, killed 7.6.15.

Wounded.   Casualties 14.6.15.
4470 Rfn W Calwell, 8768 Rfn B Coxall, R7392 Rfn H Maybury, 8862 Rfn W Parrnham.
                            Casualties 15.6.15.
Y302 Rfn J Bingham, 11011 Rfn J Prescott. Wounded
                            Casualties 16.6.15.
9830 L/c M Monk, Killed.
R9301 Rfn A Withers, R7296 Rfn S Swallow, R9435 Rfn D Williams, Y1629 Rfn J Harris, wounded.
9710 Rfn J Cook, wounded 17.6.15.
5576 Rfn J Hadingham, wounded 24.6.15.

                            Casualties 27.6.15.
Killed. 11059 Rfn W Bevereley, 8853 Rfn A Waterhouse.
Wounded R9925 L/c H.J.Phillips, Y190 Rfn E Smith.

9321 Rfn R Walker, wounded 29.6.15.

80th Infantry Brigade.
27th Division.

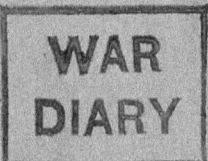

4th BATTN. THE KING'S ROYAL RIFLE CORPS.

J U L Y
(1.7.15 to 1.8.15)

1 9 1 5

Attached:
Casualty List.

4th Battalion The King's Royal Rifle Corps.

July 1915

1-7-15 — On night of 1st the battalion took over the right
sector from K.S.L.I. having battalion H.Q. in CHAPELLE
D'ARMENTIERES.

-5-7-15 — The four days were extremely uneventful, a though
which had arrived under 2nd Bays ... was
employed in two nights digging a new eaten trench.

WAR DIARY
or
INTELLIGENCE SUMMARY.
(Erase heading not required.)

Army Form C. 2118.

Instructions regarding War Diaries and Intelligence Summaries are contained in F.S. Regs., Part II. and the Staff Manual respectively. Title pages will be prepared in manuscript.

Hour, Date, Place	Summary of Events and Information	Remarks and references to Appendices
5-7-15	An endeavour to tap the enemy communications was made by Lt. BARKER and Lt. WILSON Brigade signalling officer by sending a wire close in front of our parapet. This was carried out in daylight up to only the first breastbarb emplds – The astatic lamp to put in another was on night of 6/5. 3d Battalion was relieved by the 2d Battalion on the night of 5th + went out to billets in the Asylum, a detachment of coys of A Coy + half B remaining in support. One detachment came out on night of 7 on relief going into support billets ERINETTE.	
9-7-15		

(73989) W4141—463. 400,000. 9/14. H.&J.Ltd. Forms/C. 2118/10.

Instructions regarding War Diaries and Intelligence Summaries are contained in F. S. Regs., Part II and the Staff Manual respectively. Title pages will be prepared in manuscript.

INTELLIGENCE SUMMARY.
(Erase heading not required.)

Hour, Date, Place	Summary of Events and Information	Remarks and references to Appendices
9.7.15	The Battalion took over the EPINETTE section & the Cure Ha Relief being completed 11.45 P.M.	
10.7.15	One man killed in Tr. Enemy very active working in front of his line. Owing to 2 yards of enemy blocking the wire in front of his trenches with a view to attack – Patrols went out at night to the wire lines carefully examined by day also with the result that there appears to be no changes in the wire.	
11-7-15	On this day the enemy attacking put out more wire in front of Tr. About 11 p.m. enemy sent up some Green flares followed thro' by a little artillery fire.	

INTELLIGENCE SUMMARY

(Erase heading not required.)

Hour, Date, Place	Summary of Events and Information	Remarks and references to Appendices
12th & 13th July	The 12th & 13th July were extremely quiet days. Nothing of note occurring. On night of 13th the Battalion was relieved by 4th R.B. The relief was hung up considerably owing to the enemy across at supports from one side to the other & was not completed until 12.20 A.M. 14th	
14.15.-7.-15	Went into billets in the town — forming Brigade reserve — Part of D Coy under Captain CURTIS two days in support. This detachment was relieved by another party of D & B under Lt BARKER on the night of 15/15 + they (6½ men wounded) over to 149 Bde on night of 16th - 17th.	

89

INTELLIGENCE SUMMARY.

(Erase heading not required.)

Hour, Date, Place	Summary of Events and Information	Remarks and references to Appendices
17-7-15	During the night of 17th-18th the battalion marched to bivouac near STEENWERCK - The 27th Division now forming part of the 3rd Corps + becoming part of 1st Army.	
20th-7-15	On 20th the brigade moved to other bivouacs the battalion going into a field near ERQUINGHEM. The battalion remained here until August 1st when the Brigade met more went into the front line, the battalion moving to Rue Marle in close support. Three billets were however considered to crowded in consequence of shelling so on 4 August the battalion was moved into billets near Rue des ACAVETS.	[signature]
1-8-15		

CASUALTY LIST.

7052 Rfn W Barrowcliffe,wounded 3.7.15.
A63 Rfn A Taylor,killed 4.7.15.

R7216 Rfn S Dean,wounded 6.7.15.
10973 L/c Richardson,2522 Rfn J Randon,killed 8.7.15.
R9181 Rfn E Williams,wounded 9.7.15.
4788 Rfn N Shelley,killed,10.7.15.
1748 Rfn C Caird,6461 Cpl R Wilson,wounded 12.7.15.
10515 Rfn J Lilley,wounded 13.7.15.A3084 Rfn G Smith,wounded 13.7.15.
R4689 Rfn S Vernon,killed 13.7.15.

R4203 Rfn J Messenger,wounded 31.7.15.

Total casualties to date.

	Killed	Wounded	Wounded & Missing	Missing	D.W.
Officers.	6	28	1	6	1
Other Ranks.	174	618	5	275	4

80th Infantry Brigade.

27th Division.

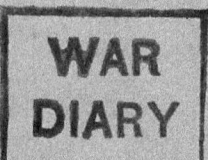

4th BATTN. THE KING'S ROYAL RIFLE CORPS.

A U G U S T

(9.8.15 to 30.8.15)

1 9 1 5

Attached:

Casualty List.

Army Form C. 2118.

WAR DIARY
or
INTELLIGENCE SUMMARY.
(Erase heading not required.)

Instructions regarding War Diaries and Intelligence Summaries are contained in F. S. Regs., Part II. and the Staff Manual respectively. Title pages will be prepared in manuscript.

Place	Date	Hour	Summary of Events and Information	Remarks and references to Appendices
ARMENTIERES	9-8-15	8 pm	The battalion moved off & relieved 3 K.R.R.C. in its left section of the 80th Inf Bde Sector. P.P.C.L.I. on our right & 50th Northumbrian Division on our left. These trenches were fairly good though chiefly of the Breastwork type. The battalion remained in for one week during the whole of which time shelling on either side was extremely slight. Heavy rain on two days made the trenches extremely wet and unpleasant more especially the new communication trenches. The "Willow" communication trenches (with floors) were soon after in strict running off. Piccadilly. During the week a great deal of work was done on the trenches making am- munition trenches, turning strikhins into french so building front foot deep outs etc — Unfortunately a radical error appeared in construction of these dug outs after the heavy rain owing to the presence of a Stratum of sand which allows the water to percolate through & eventually settling very near the lower part of the sides of the dug out caused them to collapse – We were labour who much depleted but at every rate a great amount	

INTELLIGENCE SUMMARY.

(Erase heading not required.)

Place	Date	Hour	Summary of Events and Information	Remarks and references to Appendices
			Casualties were small during the tour on 10th a lucky timed H.E. bursting over the support trenches wounded three men but not seriously. On the same day a rifleman instead of discharging his rifle killed one rifleman and wounded another, a Sgt/Cpl + 10 men arrived - On the 12th a draft of 10 men arrived. — On the evening Capt CLEMENTS and Lt BUTLER left with RFN TARRIER who was out in front of the rail to look for an emplacement for a machine gun when they were all hit. Almost certainly by the fire of certain new heavy rifles sent up to London in its trenches. During the course of this week companies of the new issue 20 + 30 rifles were attached for instruction.	
	16-8-15		On night of 15th the battalion was relieved by 3 K.R.R.C. + 2(Lond) to support at L'ARMEÉ. Being B Coy under Lt PRICE DAVIES in support. This company suffered with Captain TRAVIS (B Coy) on 19th. On 21st a shell in billets wounded eight men but only two of them were sufficiently serious to be sent away.	

INTELLIGENCE SUMMARY

(Erase heading not required.)

Place	Date	Hour	Summary of Events and Information	Remarks and references to Appendices
Nieuw ARMENTIERES TO	23.8.15	7.15 P.M.	Starting at 7.15 P.M. from bullets at L'ARMEE in their former trenches – 3 K.R.R.C. report that their relieve cavalry to have relieved Saxon infantry in our front – That their snipers are very active + good shots + that they had several casualties that day. During the night there was quite an unusual amount of rifle + machine gun fire on both sides. The whole period in the trenches has an extremely quiet one. Work was carried on continuously on the shell proof dug outs – communication trenches, Bullet proof parapets + supports + gun supporting emplacements. The left railway redoubt brought up to the trenches then was being done by support + working parties supplied by the battalions not in the trenches. The Sanillis wallis Lt. G.H. Baker made a very good job of laying out the telephone wires so arranging them that they were in position by the phones traffic to has been the case hitherto. Mr. Taylor made arrangements to daylight of the enemy's work at a diverse who a new unit south of Lille Road getting up a	G3

T2134. Wt. W708—776. 500000. 4/15. Sir J. C. & S.

INTELLIGENCE SUMMARY

(Erase heading not required.)

Place	Date	Hour	Summary of Events and Information	Remarks and references to Appendices
ditto			within 80 or 30 yards of then escaped.	
	26th		On 26th Cpl Wilkin with a patrol also in daylight brought in several copies of the GAZETTE DES ARDENNES and one copy of the LEIPZIGER NEUESTE NACHRICHTEN	
	27th		On the night of 27th a demonstration was made north the object of inducing enemy on the enemy's transport & ration parties &c.— R.F.S. fired sixteen rounds starspol + two machine guns firing fifteen in conjunction. 2 Lt J.L. CLOWES found a soft nosed bullet was fired up by the enemy not what was fired on him.	
	30th		On the morning of 30th the 18th Hargeon fired a few rounds cordite at the barricade opposite 65 French the shooting was good but there were many blind shells. In the evening the Brigade was relieved by 82nd Bde - the Royal Irish taking over from us together with one [?] company Leinsters. The relief was complete by 10·40 P.M.	

CASUALTY LIST.

Casualties for period 1st to 31st August 1915.

No.	Rank	and Name.	Nature of casualty.	
6193	Rfn	T Rowland.	Killed in action,	6.8.15.
1656	"	A Cridge.	"	"
R7391	"	W Freeman.	Wounded,	"
Y1781	"	W Parker.	"	"
R11120	"	T Chilton.	"	"
8421	L/c	H Robinson.	Accidentally killed,	10.8.15.
Y1051	"	E Bland.	" wounded,	"
R10768	Rfn	E Plamer.	Wounded,	"
4865	"	J Owen.	Wounded,	"
Y969	"	E Davies.	Wounded,	"
Captain		M.L.S.Clements.	Wounded,	13.8.15.
Lieut.		T.A. Butcher.	Wounded,	"
7937	L/c	H.Tarver.	Wounded,	"
7031	Rfn	M.Owen.	Wounded,	22.8.15.
7876	"	B.Mann.	Wounded,	"
8176	"	G.Averill.	Wounded.	"
R9479	"	A.Farraway.	Woundedd	"
7046	Sgt	J.Delaney.	Wounded,	"
7498	Rfn	T.Rose.	Wounded,	"
12217	"	W"Towse.	Wounded,	"
R5618	Sgt	G.Morgan.	Wounded.	27.8.15.

Total casualties to date.

	Killed.	Wounded.	Wounded & Miss.	Missing.	D.W
Officers.	6	30	1	6	1
Other ranks.	177	632	5	275	4

80th Infantry Brigade.
27th Division.

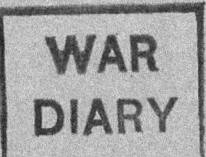

4th BATTN. THE KING'S ROYAL RIFLE CORPS.

SEPTEMBER

(31.8.15 to 30.9.15)

1 9 1 5

Attached:
Casualty List.

WAR DIARY or INTELLIGENCE SUMMARY

Place	Date	Hour	Summary of Events and Information	Remarks and references to Appendices
	31.8.15 TO 13.9.15		The battalion retired to bivouac near ERQUINGHEM bridge as before where we arrived by 11.15 p.m. The battalion remained in divisional reserve during this period. The time was occupied in drill, training etc. & several heavy digging fatigues were found in RUE FLEURIE, LA VESEE and BOIS GRENIER. On 13.9.15 A.F. whilst out route marching near STEENWERCK 4 German aeroplanes were seen fighting with a British one (which offered a stout engagement. The German appeared to be in difficulties & began to descend. The aeroplanes both a long while round & eventually met as if to alight near the battalion. The leading company got ready to fire & fool was the aviators neared the ground it started to rise again & was in hiding before fire & the aeroplane brought down itself & German being killed. Battalion marched at 6.30 P.M. & turning up with 10 sect of the Brigade bivouced 15 miles STRAZEELE	
	14.9.15			

INTELLIGENCE SUMMARY.

Place	Date	Hour	Summary of Events and Information	Remarks and references to Appendices
STRAZEELE	18.9.15		Marched to HAZEBROUCK for entrainment. The transport going on ahead. Train started at 12.9 P.M arriving at AILLOUCOURT 11.30 P.M	
	19.9.15		After detrainment the battalion marched to FRISSY about 4 miles. D Company moved up to ECLUSIER arriving at 4 P.M. w supported at 3 A.M. who took over part of the line from the French 309th Brigade. The remainder of the battalion went into huts & billets in the canal at FRISSY. The 27th Division thus came into the 12th Corps.	
	21.9.15		Battalion moved up to CAPPY going into billets — 8 platoons to form machine guns were now in the firing line in supports of 3rd KRRC + one Company in ECLUSIER in close support.	
	25.9.15		The battalion relieved the 3rd Battalion in the trenches at the same time PPCLI relieved on its left + the M.G.s.	
	26.9.15		Situation fairly quiet. a few shrapnel + rifle grenades fired into R 2 Trench the latter especially at night but the shell'd when asked to with field guns.	
	27.9.15		A very quiet day, no guns firing all day.	

INTELLIGENCE SUMMARY.

(Erase heading not required.)

Place	Date	Hour	Summary of Events and Information	Remarks and references to Appendices
	27.9.15		Towards evening the enemy showed a considerable activity with Rifle grenades & trench mortars against R1 & R2 — Several casualties were caused by rifle grenades but none by the French mortars. The mine crater in front of R2 was bombed by us during the night unfortunately, a large number of the bombs failed to ignite.	
	28.9.15		Sniping activity on part of the enemy with French mortars & Aërs bombs.	
	29.9.15		During the morning there was a further bombardment by the enemy with French howitzers + in R.2 — Howitzer fire in retaliation strongly inadequate.	
	30.9.15		Enemy very quiet — the trenches were shelled by our French howitzers & there was no retaliation except for a few rifle grenades. In the evening trench mortars started but the German battery retaliated almost immediately on they did not continue. A good deal of Rifle grenading went on against FORTIN.	

CASUALTY LIST.

Casualties for period 1st to 30th September 1915.

No.	Rank and Name.	Nature of casualty.		
Y889	Rfn S Bolton.	Accidentally killed, 13.9.1915.		
R9483	" F Roe.	Wounded, 22.9.15.		
Lieut.	F.G.de Satge.	Wounded, 25.9.15.		
29	Sgt F Featherstone.	Killed in action, 26.9.15.		
R10372	Rfn G Wright.	"	"	
Y811	" C Fox.	Wounded.	"	
R9909	" J Gilman.	"	"	
10731	" A James.	"	"	
Y309	" W Leyland.	"	"	
A585	" J Parkyn.	"	"	since dead.
Y818	" T Round.	"	"	
10510	" G Apted.	"	27.9.15.	
8738	" E Waddington.	"	28.9.15.	
7812	" C Pratt.	"	"	
7717	" J Johnson.	"	"	
R7717	" W Pearson.	"	29.9.15.	
4046	" J Swallow.	"	"	
4307	" A Langdon.	"	"	
7730	L/c O Whiteside.	"	"	
9955	Sgt E Edmunds.	"	30.9.15.	
12272	Rfn T Smith.	"	"	
403	Cpl E Morley.	"	"	

Total casualties to date.

	Killed.	Wounded.	W & Missing.	Missing.	D.W.
Officers.	6	31	1	6	1
Other ranks.	180	650	5	275	5

80th Infantry Brigade.
27th Division.

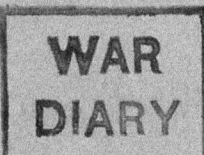

4th BATTN. THE KING'S ROYAL RIFLE CORPS.

O C T O B E R

1 9 1 5

Attached:
Appendix B.

WAR DIARY
or
INTELLIGENCE SUMMARY.
(Erase heading not required.)

Army Form C. 2118.

Place	Date	Hour	Summary of Events and Information	Remarks and references to Appendices
FRISE	1-10-15		A quiet day except for stray bombs, especially near the battalion HQrs at Montin. In the evening 3 K.R.R.C. relieved the Battalion.	
	2-10-15		After relief the battalion marched to the huts at FROISSY being all in by 11.45 p.m.	
	5-10-15		The 11th Scottish Rifles also were in huts & up for instruction with us and with 3 K.R.R.C.	
FROISSY	6-10-15		Battalion remained in FROISSY huts in reserve.	
	7-10-15		On evening of 5th The battalion took over from 3 K.R.R.C. 4 minenwerfer fell opposite in T. 3 & 2 in K.2 also about 10 whiz bangs. Otherwise all quiet.	
	8-10-15		A quiet day – During the night enemy were reported working on his front line & in front of Hamwell Wood by day. Enemy sent 4 minenwerfer into 7.3 New trench mortar fired in reply large crater about midway. Enemy replied with rifle grenades. Lt. M.E. ANTROBUS hit whilst near Bois de la Vache	
	9-10-15		A quiet day until evening when enemy fired a few minenwerfer into K.2 & K.3 on our left.	

T2134. Wt. W708–776. 500000. 4/15. Sir J. C. & S.

Instructions regarding War Diaries and Intelligence
Summaries are contained in F.S. Regs., Part II.
and the Staff Manual respectively. Title pages
will be prepared in manuscript.

INTELLIGENCE SUMMARY.
(Erase heading not required.)

Place	Date	Hour	Summary of Events and Information	Remarks and references to Appendices
FRISE	9.10.15		In Evening the battalion was relieved by 3 K.R.R.C. The Battalion arriving in billets in CAPPY at 9.45 P.M	
CAPPY.	11.10.15		During the tour the 10th DEVONS were attached for 48 hours for instruction	Reference to app.
			On 11th The Battalion marched at 2 P.M. to MORCOURT arriving there at 4.30 P.M. & coming into command of 82nd INF BDE. Temporarily	
MORCOURT.	15.10.15		Came under the command of 67th INF BDE.	
"	16.10.15	-	Marched at 12.45 P.M en route for the Trenches halting at FRISSY for Teas - Marched on again at 5.30 P.M. relieving the French Regiment in K #1, 2 & front of 3 sectors - Relief complete by 9.35. P.M	
	17.10.15		An extremely quiet day - nothing to report	
	18.10.15		Enemy put about 20 shells into the French line in the morning killing one Cameron Highlander on working party & wounding one Rifleman	
	19.10.15		Enemy put about 50 Drummenfeur (60.6) into our trenches in the morning. The reply on the part of our artillery was entirely inadequate. Enemy did a good deal of work on his line during the night	
	20.10.15		Another quiet day - the arrangements made to deal with the enemy snipers	

INTELLIGENCE SUMMARY.

(Erase heading not required.)

Place	Date	Hour	Summary of Events and Information	Remarks and references to Appendices
Trenches	25-10-15		In front of FORTIN and opposite K1 appears to be successful — Expected relief did not come off tonight owing to alteration of plans. 67th Bdes reformed as before — 20th Returned to trenches K.S.L.I. rec over from S.W.B on our right — Both Bdes H.Q took over from # 67th at CAPPY. During the night enemy put out a large amount of wire opposite K1 & K.3. on knife rests. — Our snipers again appear to completely dominate those of the enemy — This day was extremely quiet.	
FROISSY	25 evening		The 3 K.R.R.C. retired relief being complete by 7.6 P.M. The battalion went into huts in FROISSY.	
WARFUSEE-ABANCOURT	25-26/10-15 26th		The battalion bivouacked in brigade reserve at FROISSY noted 26-10-15. On 26th Battalion marched from FROISSY to WARFUSEE - ABANCOURT. The trenches having been taken over the previous night by the French	
BOVES.	27th		Continued march to BOVES & went into camp — a wet cold march.	
REVELLES.	28th		Arrived in REVELLES and went into billets — 3rd Battalion also in same village. While resting here information received of unloaded men of 27th Division	

Army Form C. 2118.

(101)

WAR DIARY
or
INTELLIGENCE SUMMARY.
(Erase heading not required.)

Instructions regarding War Diaries and Intelligence Summaries are contained in F. S. Regs., Part II. and the Staff Manual respectively. Title pages will be prepared in manuscript.

Place	Date	Hour	Summary of Events and Information	Remarks and references to Appendices
REVELLES			to Balkans. — The two battalions were inspected by General Horlock commanding 10th Corps to which we were attached. The period of rest was very profitably employed in training.	

APPENDIX B.

Appendix B.

Casualties up to 30/11/1915.

9836 Rfn F Ratcliffe.	Acc. Wounded.	1/10/15.
11746 " D Gibbins.	Wounded.	5/10/15.
Lieut. M.E.Antrobus.	"	8/10/15.
6822 " H Hall.	Killed in action.	18/10/15.
7825 L/c W Smith.	Wounded.	"
7208 Rfn J West.	"	19/10/15.
Y1778 " S Bannagan.	"	20/10/15.
Y901 " W Strickley.	"	"

Total casualties to date.

	Killed.	Wounded.	W & Missing.	Missing.	D. of W.
Officers.	6	32	1	6	1
Others.	181	656	6	275	5